ENERGY KEEPERS

ENERGY KILLERS

ENERGY KEEPERS
ENERGY KILLERS

The New Civil Rights Battle

Roy Innis

Merril Press
BELLEVUE, WASHINGTON

ENERGY KEEPERS - ENERGY KILLERS

First Edition
Published by Merril Press

Typeset by The Free Enterprise Press,
a division of The Center for the Defense of Free Enterprise.
12500 N.E. 10th Place, Bellevue, Washington 98005.
Telephone 425-455-5038. Fax 425-451-3959.
E-mail address: books@cdfe.org.
Cover design by Northwoods Studio.

ENERGY KEEPERS - ENERGY KILLERS

is published by Merril Press
P.O. Box 1682, Bellevue, Washington 98009.
Additional copies of this book may be ordered from
Merril Press at $15.00 each.
Telephone 425-454-7009.

LIBRARY OF CONGRESS CATALOGING-IN-PUBLICATION DATA
Innis, Roy, 1934-
Energy keepers energy killers : the new civil rights battle / Roy Innis. -- 1st ed.
    p. cm.   .
Includes bibliographical references and index.
ISBN-13: 978-0-936783-52-9
ISBN-10: 0-936783-52-4
1. Energy policy--United States. 2. Minorities--United States--Political activity.
3. Minorities--United States--Economic conditions. I. Title.
HD9502.U52I534 2008
333.790973--dc22

    2007048131

SECOND PRINTING
PRINTED IN THE UNITED STATES OF AMERICA

TABLE OF CONTENTS

PART ONE: ENERGY KEEPERS

PART TWO: ENERGY KILLERS

Dedication
To my family,
and to all the Energy Keepers struggling for energy civil rights.

Foreword
by
Sean Hannity

The book you are about to read will change the world. The man who wrote it will see to that. And what a remarkable man he is.

I have known Roy Innis and the Innis family for fifteen years. They have endured heartbreak, and they have experienced the joy of victory in their struggle for civil rights, for racial equality, and for economic opportunity and individual liberty for all Americans.

In those fifteen years, my admiration for Roy Innis has grown to iconic proportions. I have seen him take on those who would belittle and harm our great nation. I have marveled as he worked to make the able more able, while also giving a hand up to the poor and disadvantaged and insisting on hard work and personal responsibility. I have also watched as he literally punched out arrogance and bigotry. Roy Innis is no man to trifle with.

To me, Roy Innis is more than a man. He is a symbol of all that Americans can do, of all that we can be – if only we keep up the struggle, never lose sight of what we fight for, and never, ever give up.

But if you ask Roy Innis, he is just another American, working for economic self-reliance, suspicious of big government, not afraid to be called a patriot, and speaking out for the individual liberties of his fellow citizens. He has no illusions about how hard it is to make a difference, and how small each of us is when we face overwhelming odds alone.

In this book, *Energy Keepers - Energy Killers: The New Civil Rights Battle*, Roy has raised his sights to some truly overwhelming odds. He has targeted the huge environmental cartel of global warming zealots who would strip America of its present energy for "alternatives" that don't even exist yet. And he calls us all to join in stopping these Energy Killers before their half-baked ideas enslave us in a fatal Energy Gap. For Roy Innis also has no illusions about how great we are when we face overwhelming odds together.

He calls us to the new civil rights battle, to protect our liberty to heat our homes, to light our way, and to travel as we wish, not only for the poor and disadvantaged, but for every American.

His bottom line: Let freedom ring!

So read this book. Pass it on to others. Act on its message.

You will change the world.

THE TORCH OF FREEDOM

THE TORCH OF ENERGY

THE TORCH OF ECONOMIC CIVIL RIGHTS

Introduction
by
Alan Gottlieb

It is an honor to help in the publication of Roy Innis's book, *Energy Keepers - Energy Killers: The New Civil Rights Battle*. Coming from an icon of the American civil rights movement – the Chairman of the Congress of Racial Equality, or CORE – this book is destined to spark the real energy debate:

Where are the BTUs?

BTUs are a measure of energy, and Roy Innis has had the grit to say in this book that there's no real, measurable energy in all the so-called "energy plans" coming out of Congress, the states and the candidates.

That is a serious problem for all Americans, but most of all for the disadvantaged, the poor and minorities – the very people whose civil rights get trampled the most. They need heat to cook with and keep the cold away, light to see by, electricity to run their appliances, fuel to power their vehicles, fuel for their employers, hospitals and kids' schools.

The government doesn't have an obligation to *give* energy to its citizens – we don't have a constitutional right to free energy – but our leaders certainly have the obligation allow us access to energy that belongs to us and we're willing to pay for. The have absolutely no right to keep available energy away from us in the name of their political agenda, be it to stop global warming, create a progressive new society for the 21st Century, foster world peace, or "protect" millions of acres that "just happen" to be located on top of our richest oil, gas, coal and uranium prospects.

But that's exactly what's happening now, and that's what Roy Innis has written about so eloquently in *Energy Keepers - Energy Killers*.

Our leaders and their political allies in "social change" movements have decided that we can't have the energy to run our lives, because most of it is fossil fuels, which cause global warming, which will end the world. So you can't use them anymore – even though those fuels supply 85% of our energy, and there are serious questions about global warming that the true believers won't answer, and don't want anyone even to ask.

Instead, our political leaders tell us, we must immediately change to "clean energy" – wind and solar. But Roy Innis shows us that, in 2006, wind and solar combined gave us less than one-half of one percent of the energy America consumed. That leaves a huge energy gap, a yawning chasm, between the real energy we have or need – and the futuristic, make-believe energy that our leaders keep promising will "transform" our nation.

In the face of this huge energy gap, our leaders insist on stopping America's domestic oil and gas production, eradicating petroleum operations from federal lands, restricting the use of coal, further delaying nuclear power plants, and imposing ridiculous "cap-and-trade" schemes that will do nothing but price the poor out of heat, light and travel, in the name of reducing industrial emissions.

That's where the real civil rights battle lies. No government, no social change movement and no ideologue has the right to take that fossil fuel energy away from us. The federal lands belong to the poor and disadvantaged, as much as to some foundation-funded environmental executive, some ambitious influence peddler gone to Washington to get marble dust in his veins, or some elected official who thinks she's an energy empress.

This theft of the people's energy has angered Roy Innis deeply. But he has learned through a lifetime of tragedy and triumph to channel anger into creative paths, to take the bad and make it good. He has endured the most horrible and horrifying personal heartbreak – the loss of his first son Roy, Jr. to criminal gunfire at the age of 13 in 1968, and then his next oldest son Alexander, who was shot and slain in 1982, at the age of 26. The pain and grief are unimaginable to me.

Yet Roy did not reactively blame the guns, but became a champion of armed self-defense against criminals with guns. Instead of drowning in bitterness, which would be all too easy under the circumstances, Roy Innis became a nationally known advocate of Second Amendment rights.

And that is the path Roy Innis sees for himself in the energy debate. Don't blame the energy companies. Instead, become an advocate for energy rights against the real culprits: the politicians, the activists, the ideologues – who would take our rights from us, and consign us to energy and economic deprivation.

Roy Innis tells it like it is, and offers strategies to counter the Energy Killers, as he aptly calls them, who would force us into a deadly energy gap, where the long promised "energy of tomorrow" is not there today, and the tangible energy of today has been taken from us. He suggests ways we can help the Energy Providers do the best job possible with the real energy we have now.

This book is not just a critique of the problem. It is a handbook for the solution: to call together all people of good will as Energy Keepers, to do the best they can, to conserve energy where they can, and to join in the fight to keep our American energy production flowing.

His ideas are stunning, his book is marvelous.

It is my great pleasure to give the world *Energy Keepers - Energy Killers: The New Civil Rights Battle*, by Roy Innis.

Alan Gottlieb
Center for the Defense of Free Enterprise
Bellevue, Washington

x

Author's Preface
by
Roy Innis

This book is about energy – *your* energy.

It's about what you cook with, how you heat your home, what makes your television work, how you get places, what makes your job possible, what runs your whole world. It's about money – more money every day, it seems. A tank of gas, utility bills, a bag of groceries, all give us ever-growing money pain.

And it's about injustice. High utility bills are a leading cause of homelessness. Just getting to work every day eats up more and more of our income. Higher energy costs force companies to lay off workers. Some must then choose between heating and eating.

Energy is the "master resource," the foundation for everything else. Abundant, reliable, affordable electricity, natural gas and transportation fuels make our jobs, health and living standards possible.

Energy is the great equalizer, the creator of economic opportunities and true environmental justice.

Push energy prices up and everybody suffers. When energy costs too much, industry lays people off, or just leaves. Jobs, incomes and tax revenues vanish. Government social programs wither. Talent and leadership migrate, to other cities or other countries. Social ills multiply.

Who gets hurt first? The poor and disadvantaged. And we all know that racial and ethnic minorities include more than our fair share of the poor and disadvantaged. We don't need energy racism. Destroy jobs, make poor families pay ever larger chunks of their meager incomes for energy – and our hard-won victories for voting and other civil rights quickly crumble to dust.

That's why I say the fight over energy is the critical civil rights battle of our era. It's not Jena, symbolic nooses, or derogatory language. It's *energy*.

And that's why I wrote this book. America's energy is in danger.

Your utility bills, the price you pay at the pump, your job security, are in danger – and not just because of Middle East oil wars or competition from China and India. Our rights are being endangered because of what's happening right here at home.

What am I talking about?

I'm talking about well-funded, aggressive, deceptive campaigns that are gathering steam right now, threatening jobs, budgets and families by *shutting down energy production on American soil.*

I'm talking about new "hunting and fishing groups" that spend little time or money enjoying the outdoors – and a lot of it *fighting against oil, gas and coal production right here in America.*

xi

I'm talking about affluent environmental groups that look for the best places to drill for oil and gas or mine for coal, and deliberately pressure politicians to stick them in energy graveyards they call "wilderness" areas, where they've buried *decades* worth of energy – *your* energy.

I'm talking about foundations that give millions to these zealots every year, to slow or stop production of *your* energy on *your* public lands.

Choke off energy supplies, and energy prices go up, and up.

Even Congress can't repeal the law of supply and demand.

And what about Congress?

Some politicians are demanding higher mileage from cars that then have to be made smaller, lighter and less safe – costing more *lives* every year.

These elitist policy makers are deciding how you should live your life – what kind of house you should have, what kind of car you should drive, what kind of vacation you should take and how you can get there – and even what standard of living you "deserve."

They cause poor families to lose their homes. They make life tougher for families who've worked, struggled and sacrificed to join the middle class. Then they throw out crumbs that make us beggars at the American banquet.

Their bottom line?

They don't want you to have abundant, reliable, affordable energy.

They believe what activist Jeremy Rifkin said about adequate, affordable energy: "It's the worst thing that could happen to our planet!"

They believe what biologist Paul Ehrlich said about adequate, affordable energy: "It would be like giving a machine gun to an idiot child."

Are you the "idiot child" he's talking about? Yes. Am I? Yes.

All of us are that "idiot child." All of us that don't share their wealth, their views, their power over others – *or their bigotry.*

That kind of prejudice has got to be stopped.

It's popular to blame it all on price gouging by big corporations. But what about the nearly 50 cents in taxes stuck on a gallon of gas today?

That's *government* price gouging.

What about stacks and stacks of dubious environmental rules? The costs are so well hidden we can only guess what they add to our utility bills.

That's *regulatory* price gouging.

What about the huge federal land areas out West with years worth of oil, gas, coal, nuclear and other energy resources that have been placed off limits? That's *our* energy. When we can't develop it, we have to import more from countries that don't like us, and pay more for it.

That's *environmentalist* price gouging.

And what about legislation that forces us to use politically correct "renewable" energy, like wind and solar, that's expensive, unreliable, land-gobbling, and unable to produce enough fuel or electricity for a modern society?

That's *ideological* price gouging.

That's bad enough. But politicians also want to force families to pay thousands of dollars a year to "stop global warming" with "cap-and-trade" schemes that cost devastating millions. You can argue about global warming, but there is no argument about the cost of political global warming tactics.

German consumers found that out the hard way, when "cap-and-trade" laws sent their utility bills soaring 25 percent in 2007. Chancellor Angela Merkel's advisor, Lars Josefsson, dismissed the hardships. Higher electricity prices, he said, are "the *intent* of the whole exercise. If there were no effects, why should you have a cap-and-trade system?"

They *want* to make energy more expensive and less available!

They're waging a war against energy – against *us*. We have to defend ourselves. But how? We can't force companies to produce more energy.

We don't have the millions that anti-energy campaigners use to stop companies from producing more energy. We don't make the laws, we don't have an army of lobbyists, we don't have big foundation donors.

But we do have the power to resist injustice. If somebody is trying to take our heat, light, jobs and travel away from us, we have the right and the duty to resist. We have a right to sit at the energy lunch counter – to not be forced to sit at the back of the energy bus

We can, and must make our voices heard, in no uncertain terms.

We can, and must tell those anti-energy activists and politicians: This is *our* energy. These are *our* jobs. These are *our* families. And we won't stand for this injustice anymore.

We can, and must block them every time they try to stop energy producers from doing their job: providing us with the energy we need to live.

There are three key players in this new civil rights battle:

There are people who produce energy for everything we do, everything we buy, everything we dream of – **The Energy Providers**.

There are people who try to stop them: activists and politicians against oil and gas drilling, against coal mining, against nuclear power, against *all* energy production, choking off the abundant, reliable, affordable American resources we need – **The Energy Killers**.

And there are people like you and me. We must unite and protect ourselves from the Energy Killers. We need to demand more energy, not less. We need to demand a seat at the lunch counter, at the front of the bus, at the table where decisions are made. We need to demand that the Energy Killer campaigns end – that the Energy Killers stop cutting off our supplies, stop pricing us out of the American Dream, and stop violating our basic civil rights. We need to be **The Energy**

Acknowledgments

My thanks to everyone who helped put this book together, first, to my editor Paul Driessen, who not only encouraged me every step of the way, but also did a vast amount of research and fact checking with many, many experts.

My thanks to Alan Gottlieb, founder of Merril Press, for accepting this book for publication and for granting permission to reprint certain vital graphics from earlier Merril Press publications, and to Ron Arnold, of the Free Enterprise Press, who managed the layout and production process for Merril, and asked many questions that needed an answer.

Particular thanks go to the technical experts in the energy industry, non-profit groups, academia and Congress who provided research materials and then fielded my questions or reviewed draft chapters. Richard Ranger of the American Petroleum Institute provided national statistics and referrals to specialists in the field; Marc Smith of the Independent Petroleum Association of Mountain States, supplied facts and figures on the independent oil and gas sector; Marita Noon of the Citizens Alliance for Responsible Energy provided the essay "Energy Utopia," which led to many good ideas; Marc Morano, staff member of the Senate Committee on Environment and Public Works, provided numerous world media clips on global warming; John R. Christy, of the Earth System Science Center at the University of Alabama in Huntsville, reviewed portions of the draft; John Goodman of the National Center for Policy Analysis gave permission to use graphics from *A Global Warming Primer*.

The opinions expressed in this book are not necessarily those of the people who so generously gave of their time and knowledge. Any errors of fact or judgment must be solely attributed to me.

PART 1

ENERGY KEEPERS

CHAPTER 1
THE ENERGY PROBLEM

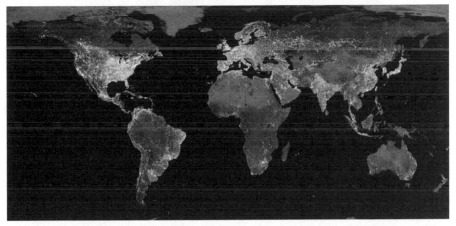

Our Earth at night is a sobering, eye-opening image. Modern cities twinkle across a darkened planet, attesting to the myriad ways energy and technology have transformed our lives – and have given even poor citizens blessings beyond what kings and queens enjoyed just a century ago.

And yet, look at the picture above.

Vast areas remain dark across the continents, where millions of families still depend on human and animal muscle, wood and animal dung, to sustain their fragile existence. When the sun goes down, their lives shut down.

To a scientist, the simplest technical definition of energy is "the ability to do work."

The "work" may appear as mechanical motion, heat, light, electricity, chemical reactions, even the thermonuclear blaze of the stars. It's all energy.

But to everyone, including scientists, energy is much more than that. It is the creator of opportunity, health and prosperity ... the maker of dreams come true ... the "master resource" that makes our jobs, lives and living standards possible.

Look around you. Try to imagine what your home, community and life would be like without abundant, reliable, affordable energy. For lights and refrigerators, computers and televisions, schools and hospitals, offices, shops and factories, food, transportation and countless other marvels that improve, enrich and safeguard our lives.

Simply put, energy transforms the civil rights enshrined in our Constitution into civil rights we enjoy in reality. Energy is our nation's life-blood, the mostly unseen but ever-present force that powers our economic engine and creates opportunities and living standards that are the envy of the world. It is the sustenance we take for granted – until disaster cuts its flow.

1

A mere half century ago, our civil rights battles were over literacy tests, voting rights, and laws that barred minorities from buses, restaurants and schools. We won that struggle.

Today we face a more subtle, but no less insidious, threat to our liberties – and this threat will oppress everyone, not only minorities and the disadvantaged as in the past.

Today we must confront a new kind of imperialism: people, political figures and organizations that would curtail our energy supplies – and thus our personal, economic and civil rights – to satisfy their ideological version of "saving the Earth." We must win this struggle, too.

America and the world have two choices in the raging debate over energy, environment and catastrophic climate change.

Will we have the energy we need, when we need it, at prices we can afford?

Or won't we?

Put another way: Amid all the fuss we hear about the need to slash greenhouse gas emissions and switch to "clean" energy sources, to prevent hypothetical climate change and other "catastrophes," the disadvantaged need ask only two questions about the "solutions" that environmental alarmists offer:

1. Do those "solutions" provide more energy – or less?
2. Do they lower the cost of energy – or raise it?

If they provide less energy, or raise the cost of energy, many dis-advantaged families will have to choose between heating and eating. Many will freeze jobless in the dark, as I testified to Congress in 2007.

For the disadvantaged, life really is that simple. Even for the middle class, life is getting there, and America's eco-imperialists are helping it along.

But if you pose those questions to alarmists like Al Gore or the Sierra Club, you won't get a straight answer. They'll change the subject.

They'll scream at you for using fossil fuels – oil, gasoline, natural gas, coal – because, they insist, those fuels cause pollution when you use them.

They won't listen when you tell them those fuels heat your home and run your car and give you a job. Or that our cars and power plants are 90 percent cleaner than just 35 years ago. Or that your fuels are real – whereas theirs exist only in tiny amounts, and in the dreams of get-rich-quick artists chasing after new government subsidies.

They'll insist that fossil fuels will melt icecaps, raise sea levels and destroy our planet. They'll ignore the total lack of evidence for these disasters, and the much more likely catastrophe that you will lose your job and your home if their recommendations become law.

They'll call you selfish and short-sighted – and say your self-indulgence will leave a legacy of pollution and planetary chaos for your children.

But don't bother telling them about your energy needs. They don't care about you. They don't have to. They're political and energy power brokers. You're politically insignificant. For now, anyway.

Until you learn a few basics, and tell *them* a few things – about energy and civil rights. Then they'll *have* to listen.

What do you have to know?

Let's look at the most basic, cold, hard facts.

America used about 100 quadrillion BTUs of energy in 2007. That's British Thermal Units, a common energy measurement. One BTU is the energy you need to raise a pound of water one degree Fahrenheit. But all you need to remember is that 100 quadrillion BTUs is *a lot* of energy.

So where does your energy come from? That's the most important question. I'm talking about *all* our energy, transportation, electrical, *the whole thing*. Here are the facts – what we might call the Energy Reality chart:

Fossil fuels – 84.9% of all the energy Americans use
- 39.8 % comes from petroleum
- 22.6 % comes from coal
- 22.5 % comes from natural gas

Nuclear electricity – 8.2% of our energy is from nuclear power plants

Renewable energy – 6.9% of our juice is renewable, but:
- 3.3 % is biomass (ethanol, biodiesel, waste wood and garbage)
- 2.9 % is from hydroelectric power dams
- 0.3 % is geothermal
- 0.3 % is wind
- 0.1 % is solar and photovoltaic

Remember, this is *all* our energy, not just electricity or motor fuel. Notice that the "clean energy sources" most loudly touted in the media, wind and solar, provide *less than one half of one percent* of our energy needs.

We are 85% reliant on fossil fuels! If we abandon fossil fuels, then nuclear and renewables combined could supply only 15% of our needs.

Where would we get all that missing energy?

Certainly not from wind and solar with their tiny ½ of one percent.

Certainly not from hydroelectric dams at 2.9 percent. And that figure is likely to go down, not up, because a group that calls itself American Rivers and its super-rich ally, the **Heinz Center for Science, Economics and the Environment**, want to do away with them in a long-term dam removal campaign to prevent alleged ecological damage to fish runs and river health.

Certainly not from nuclear power's 8.2 percent contribution. And don't forget those eminent scientists disguised as entertainers – Jackson Browne, Graham Nash and Bonnie Raitt – who delivered a petition to the Senate in late 2007 denouncing nuclear energy as unsafe.

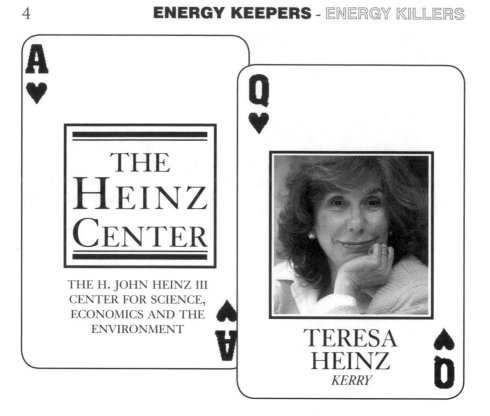

THE HEINZ CENTER

THE H. JOHN HEINZ III
CENTER FOR SCIENCE,
ECONOMICS AND THE
ENVIRONMENT

TERESA HEINZ
KERRY

I know what's best for you, Hon
Because I'm rich and you're not

Ketchup heiress and Heinz widow Teresa Heinz Kerry created the anti-energy Heinz Center with a $20 million grant in 1994.

Teresa's personal fortune is estimated at $1 billion.

Teresa not only likes dam removal, her Center generously gives cash rewards to individuals who support her policies and political agendas. It gave a $250,000 Heinz Award in the Environment to NASA employee James E. Hansen, for his "leadership in the debate over global warming," shortly after he endorsed Teresa's husband, John Kerry, for President.

She and the Center also oppose the use of insecticides to prevent malaria and other diseases that kill millions every year – arguing that a ban is vital to ending the "devastating triple whammy" that country club women get from "the chemical soup" of birth control pills, makeup and sunblock, and "daily games of golf" on courses that are "perfectly manicured," thanks to estrogenic pesticides. Her issues are certainly at the top of the list for impoverished African women who are stricken repeatedly by diseases that are also killing their babies.

Certainly not from biomass and its 3.3 percent share. Wood waste, ethanol, and biodiesel just can't do it, and *Rolling Stone* ran a long article that denounced ethanol as a hopeless, environmentally harmful energy source. (Imagine how its hip readers must have reacted to *those* inconvenient truths.)

Environmentalists don't really even like geothermal energy (less than half a percent). In the United States, it's mostly in places like Yellowstone, Mt. Lassen and Hawaii Volcanoes National Parks, and they won't tolerate having energy development within sight of a national park.

In short, certainly not from "renewables."

A lousy 6.9% won't do much – even though "renewables" always seem to be advertised as "alternatives" to fossil fuels.

The cold, hard fact is all that so-called "alternative energy" is really only "supplementary energy" – energy that's nice to have, important to America's energy mix, but no alternative. Not now, and not for a long time.

You want the truth? Try *Facing the Hard Truths About Energy,* a report from the National Petroleum Council, which is a federal advisory committee to the Secretary of Energy. It flatly says:

> • Coal, oil, and natural gas will remain indispensable to meeting total projected energy demand growth.
> • The world is not running out of energy resources, but there are accumulating risks to continuing expansion of oil and natural gas production from the conventional sources relied upon historically. These risks create significant challenges to meeting projected energy demand.
> • To mitigate these risks, expansion of all economic energy sources will be required, including coal, nuclear, renewables, and unconventional oil and natural gas. Each of these sources faces significant challenges – including safety, environmental, political, or economic hurdles – and imposes infrastructure requirements for development and delivery.
> • "Energy Independence" should not be confused with strengthening energy security. The concept of energy independence is not realistic in the foreseeable future, whereas U.S. energy security can be enhanced by moderating demand, expanding and diversifying domestic energy supplies, and strengthening global energy trade and investment. There can be no U.S. energy security without global energy security.
> • A majority of the US energy sector workforce, including skilled scientists and engineers, is eligible to retire within the next decade. The workforce must be replenished and trained.
> • Policies aimed at curbing CO_2 emissions will alter the energy mix, increase energy-related costs, and require reductions in demand growth.

Hard truths. And complicated. But not beyond comprehension.

Just that simple chart, showing what percentage of our energy really came from which source, is *a vital protection against hype.*

And it's free. I got it from a web page of the United States Energy Information Agency. Your tax dollars are already showing us Energy Reality.

That's important. Even the best analysts talk in statistics that cloud the issue, like "US ethanol production averaged 316,000 barrels a day in 2006, up 19% from 2005 levels." I checked that claim out, and it's true.

But – is that a lot? Even with this "big" increase, ethanol is still less than *half of one percent* of our energy needs. Only 99.5% to go.

Hype is everywhere. First they called it global warming. But sometimes the planet didn't behave as scripted. So they switched to "climate change." That way they could blame everything on humans.

We don't need to fall for hype. Just read the Energy Reality chart.

There's a revealing article on the "global energy crisis" in the AAA magazine, *Journey,* for November/December 2007.

It asked, "Of all the solutions that have been proposed in Congress or by U.S. presidential candidates to promote U.S. energy independence, which is the best one?"

The answer:

"The reality is that no single solution that has been proposed will lead to a decrease in U.S. gasoline consumption or achieve U.S. energy independence. Eliminating 12 million barrels a day of oil imports from our daily lives is not plausible."

Absolutely correct. Then it asked, "What should we be looking for in a sound policy on reducing reliance on foreign oil and protecting the global climate?" Answer:

"It is going to take a portfolio of polices including many different kinds of measures to reduce oil use and promote new technology. It may also require changes in lifestyle and perhaps, depending on circumstances in the future, personal sacrifices."

A portfolio of policies? Yes, that's sound. Obviously, no single policy will lead to energy independence and abundant, affordable supplies.

But what about those "changes in lifestyle" and "personal sacrifices?" That has an ominous Stone Age ring about it. What kind of lifestyle changes and personal sacrifices? Who will "get to" make them? And who decides?

Abandoning fossil fuels would leave America with an ENERGY GAP of 85% – a monstrous chasm between what we need and what we would have.

Even a fraction of that gap would mean the collapse of the American economy and the end of American society as we know it.

If we don't fill that energy gap before we cripple fossil fuel use with devastating penalties disguised as "lifestyle changes" and "protections for the global climate," those "personal sacrifices" will turn out to be national economic suicide, especially for the disadvantaged.

The Energy Killers say we use too much energy, and we won't voluntarily change our "evil" ways. In their view, the best way to make us change is to lock our energy resources up in "protected" areas, and use climate Armageddon and other environmental scare stories to justify raising prices and preventing us from using fossil fuels.

You won't see Al Gore or the Hollywood set stop using 20 times more electricity than the average American or stop flying all over the planet in private jets. You'll never see them volunteer to live in an African mud hut or even an Appalachian cabin, in the "eco-friendly" lifestyles they extol and want to perpetuate – for *you*.

But they believe they have a right to tell you and other less fortunate folks how to live. They just figure they are special. They can buy "carbon offset" indulgences, to make up for their self-gratifying life styles. And it's up to the rest of us to do the heavy lifting that's needed to Save Planet Earth.

Don't ever forget: The cost of energy affects the cost of growing, processing, manufacturing and shipping every product you buy.

The cost of energy affects the cost of every service you use.

Every one of these anti-energy proposals will increase your energy bills – and all your other bills – by hundreds or thousands of dollars a year.

Every dollar increase in your energy bills sends you further back on the economic bus.

So again I ask:

Will you have a seat at the energy and economic lunch counter?

Will you be able to afford lunch at the lunch counter?

And perhaps to the most fundamental point: Will you have a seat at the corporate, congressional and environmentalist table where these decisions are being made for you?

These are hard questions. They demand hard, honest answers.

That is why we must **keep and protect** fossil fuel use – and not demonize it. Why we must make sure we bridge the Energy Gap with real (not imaginary) "clean energy," before we take drastic steps that penalize fossil fuel use.

And why we must make sure we don't destroy the energy system we have – including fossil fuel, hydroelectric and nuclear power – before we try running our cars, homes, hospitals and industries on imaginary energy ... and burying real supplies in energy graveyards.

That is the job of The Energy Keepers.

CHAPTER 2
THE POLITICAL PROBLEM

American politics have changed. Presidential candidates don't hide or play down their environmental credentials any more.

Back in 2000, presidential wannabe Al Gore wouldn't talk about his book *Earth in the Balance*, which said the environment must become "the central organizing principle of society." He knew that if the environment were "central," *you* wouldn't be, your dreams wouldn't be, and the Bill of Rights and Fourteenth Amendment would protect the environment more than people. He also knew voters were smart enough to figure that out.

Even in 2004, John Kerry practically flinched when he got an early endorsement from the League of Conservation Voters, because of the huge media flap it caused. His wife Teresa Heinz Kerry was a board member of Environmental Defense, a big player in the League. Everybody figured her vast ketchup fortune and support of environmental causes had bought the endorsement – as they suspected her $250,000 award to global warming alarmist James Hansen had rewarded his scare-mongering and endorsement of Kerry. So he played it down.

But consider 2008. Democrats and even a lot of Republicans are falling all over each other to be the candidate of energy and global warming. The "tectonic shift" partly reflects a Democratic poll showing that 29% of respondents cite energy independence and global warming as America's most important domestic challenge, second only to health care.

The poll may be real, but it also reflects the constant drumbeat of ecological catastrophe in our media and political circles, continual domestic and international efforts to pillory President George Bush and the United States, and the literally billions of dollars that have been spent in recent years to demonize fossil fuels and promote renewable energy and climate chaos claims.

Suddenly, the environment had crossover appeal. It could even help to win over suburban Republican women, who tend to place a high priority on environmental issues. Or so the smart political strategists think. And the media report it, because it further supports their viewpoints and objectives.

I'm not so sure how real this shift is. American politics may have changed – at least for the moment, at least in the minds of the chattering classes and political in-crowd. As they say in Washington: the facts don't matter; perception matters.

But Washington remains that little Fantasyland on the banks of the Potomac River. The old joke is still new: Washington, DC is a ten-square-mile island of politicians completely surrounded by Reality. And out in the hinterlands, a basic kind of common sense still holds sway, in families where jobs, mortgage payments, food on the table, school, taxes and dreams of a better future are still top tier issues. They know our air and water quality is better, and they haven't yet been convinced that we're literally driving ourselves to a climate change calamity.

The fact is, most candidates are only rarely on speaking terms with the underlying truth of the American condition. They just believe the media buzz and pollsters' snapshot analyses – which often reflect carefully scripted questions and facts just as carefully selected to support previously staked-out positions: write the answers first, then ask the questions

They haven't examined the Energy Reality chart, and probably never even saw it. Worse, they rely on "studies," computer models and cherry-picked data from environmental lobbyists, government scientists whose paychecks depend on government appropriations, and fat-cat political contributors whose environmental ideologies are frequently contradicted by their personal lifestyles.

The numbers in government reports like this 2006 chart from the US Energy Information Administration (below) indicate that renewables won't be generating vast amounts of electricity by 2030, and it's hard to imagine them doing much more by 2050 – **Al Gore** (opposite) to the contrary.

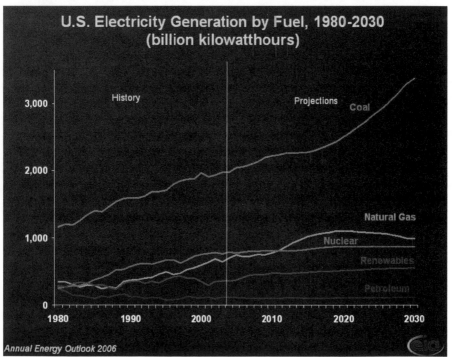

U.S. Electricity Generation by Fuel, 1980-2030
(billion kilowatthours)

Annual Energy Outlook 2006

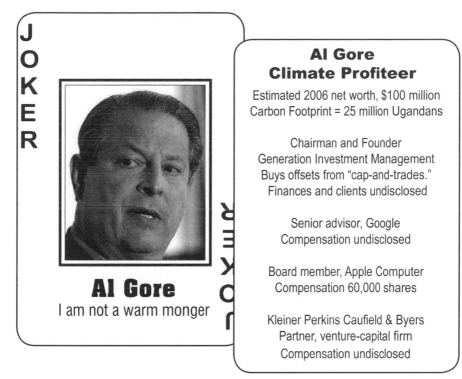

J O K E R

Al Gore

I am not a warm monger

Al Gore
Climate Profiteer

Estimated 2006 net worth, $100 million
Carbon Footprint = 25 million Ugandans

Chairman and Founder
Generation Investment Management
Buys offsets from "cap-and-trades."
Finances and clients undisclosed

Senior advisor, Google
Compensation undisclosed

Board member, Apple Computer
Compensation 60,000 shares

Kleiner Perkins Caufield & Byers
Partner, venture-capital firm
Compensation undisclosed

Cleaning Up - But Not the Environment.

Won the 2007 trifecta – Oscar, Emmy, Nobel.
Raked in undisclosed piles of cash from corporate positions and various investments, as well as speaking fees to die for.
Declined to run for President of the United States in 2008, because it would stop him from getting all that money.
In 2007 a group said his mansion in a posh area of Nashville, Tennessee consumes more electricity every month than the average American household uses in an entire year. Gore's staff didn't deny it, but justified it by saying that Gore's carbon offsets made him "carbon neutral." In other words, he didn't stop sinning against the environment; he bought his way into climate heaven, by getting free carbon indulgences from his company.
Gore accepted his Oscar with a speech about global warming: "It's not a political issue; it's a moral issue." Yes, it is – and politicians are immorally, knowingly and deliberately using the issue to drive up energy prices beyond people's ability to pay, deny Third World nations the right to generate electricity, and offer welfare subsidies to those they harm most, turning them into permanent beggars.

But politicians still emphasize their single-minded commitment to slashing greenhouse gas emissions … changing the way we Americans light our homes, fuel our automobiles and do our jobs … and forcing us to spend "billions of dollars in the short term, but potentially saving even more in the decades to follow," supposedly preventing climate catastrophes.

Then they promise to ease the pain for those of us least able to afford their prescriptions for economic suicide. They promise that the money raised by levying carbon taxes on everything we buy – or by auctioning off pollution credits in "cap-and-trade" schemes – won't just be earmarked for some new pork barrel project. It will be "invested" in research into technologies to replace the ones they are destroying, job training for people they will send to the unemployment lines, $10,000 tax credits for consumers who buy cleaner vehicles, and subsidies "for those hit hardest by rising electric bills."

Remember what Einstein said: "If we knew what we were doing, it wouldn't be called research, would it?"

In other words, they plan to enslave us all with policies that are based on unproven, over-hyped eco-Armageddon theories negotiated by government scientists – and then throw us some charity crumbs from the banquet table that they will keep well provisioned for themselves and their supporters.

These politicians never ran a company, never had to make payroll, can't do basic math or solve simple engineering problems, and in most cases never even had a real job. But suddenly they are experts on our complex (formerly) free-market economy, and have the wisdom to pick the winners and losers in our future Green Economy, under their 25 Year Plan and Great Leap Forward to a "sustainable future."

Preventing catastrophic climate change, said the *Washington Post* "will require a wholesale transformation of the nation's economy and society."

I'm not ready to have my economy, my life, my freedom and my civil rights "transformed," and placed under the control of the Climate Change Police. Are you?

And I don't think there is anything "morally responsible" about economic suicide – especially when it is imposed by well-off elites on people in lower socio-economic classes.

Unfortunately, it looks like I'm going to have a hard time finding a regulator or political candidate who shares my views on these bread-and-butter issues and the vital role of fossil fuels in our economy.

We've been hearing a lot about the horrible "pollutant" called carbon dioxide – CO2, for short. It's a big deal. Before getting much further into CO2 politics, I'd like to bring you a word from the makers of CO2: *all the animals and people on Earth.*

It's an elementary school lesson we seem totally oblivious of. Animals breathe in oxygen from the air and we breathe out carbon dioxide – CO2.

Plants do the opposite: they breathe in CO_2 from the air and breathe out oxygen. Oxygen and CO_2 go round and round in a big cycle, plants and animals, animals and plants.

However, our government, in its infinite wisdom, has declared CO_2 a *pollutant*. It's a *greenhouse gas*, meaning it holds heat in the atmosphere, and that could contribute to global warming. But how much CO_2 is there? Total CO_2 in our atmosphere is equivalent to less than 2 inches on a 100-yard football field. The human contribution is less than a third of that.

To presume that this tiny bit of carbon dioxide is the only or primary force behind climate change – more powerful than the sun, cosmic rays, clouds and other forces put together – is simply not supported by common sense or scientific evidence.

In fact, the most important greenhouse gas of all is *water vapor*. It's 95% of all greenhouse gases, and it's also a primary by-product of burning all fossil fuels. Will Congress and the EPA now propose to put a plastic lid over all bodies of water on the planet, to keep that "pollutant" from increasing?

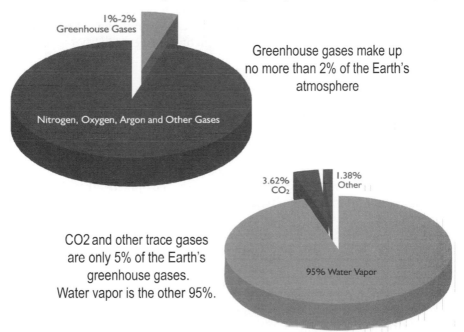

1%-2% Greenhouse Gases

Nitrogen, Oxygen, Argon and Other Gases

Greenhouse gases make up no more than 2% of the Earth's atmosphere

3.62% CO₂

1.38% Other

95% Water Vapor

CO2 and other trace gases are only 5% of the Earth's greenhouse gases. Water vapor is the other 95%.

National Center for Policy Analysis

Sure, EPA could decide not to penalize people, animals, personal vehicles, private jets and environmentalist offices that emit carbon dioxide (and water vapor), or use fossil fuels for their electricity. It could just go after power plants, commercial aircraft, factories and other selected targets that it dislikes – just as police can decide to target only red cars, or only cars going 12 mph above the posted limit. But that doesn't change the fact that this entire pollution control effort, and the rationale behind it, is arbitrary, capricious and economically harmful.

The Climate Police will get you for DWH – Driving While Human.

If CO_2 is a pollutant, that makes you and me and our dogs and cats, cows and horses, and everything else that qualifies as an animal – a pollution source. You and me, when we exhale, *we're official pollution sources*.

The US Supreme Court recently ruled that the US Environmental Protection Agency has the authority to regulate CO_2 and its sources. Nobody seems to have noticed the implication that the EPA has been given authority to regulate your breathing and mine – and our cars, homes, heating, cooling, lighting, refrigeration, and everything else that improves, safeguards and enriches our lives.

It's not that I don't trust the EPA, it's that I don't trust the people who run the EPA.

I certainly hope that common sense prevails. But I look at the EPA's track record for common sense: it once declared a springtime puddle between the tracks of a railroad in a little Idaho town to be a "wetland" and part of "the waters of the United States" – and thus subject to heavy-handed regulation. So I worry about receiving a Notice of Noncompliance and Order to Reduce Your CO_2 Emissions to Pre-1990 Levels.

In other words, the EPA could tell us: Inhale, but don't exhale.

As we are about to see, that would be a good rule for our politicians. But not for us.

Former senator John Edwards (North Carolina) pronounced that "it's time for a president who asks Americans to be patriotic about something other than war." He wants you to be patriotic about slashing greenhouse gases some 80% by 2050. "No matter what the politics are," he opined, "there's a moral responsibility to address this issue. We've got to do it." Wave the flag.

Senator Hillary Rodham Clinton too supports cutting CO_2 emissions 80% by 2050. Part of her plan would require that US vehicles average 55 miles per gallon by 2030 (the stick). Another would provide $20 billion in "Green Vehicle Bonds" to help the auto industry produce more efficient cars (the carrot).

"This is the biggest challenge we've faced in a generation," she asserted. Global warming is "a challenge to our economy, our security, our health and our planet. I believe America is ready to take action, ready to break the bonds of the old energy economy, and ready to prove that the climate crisis is also one of the greatest economic opportunities in the history of our country. It will be a new beginning for the 21st century."

Her policy skills have been praised by none other than the multi-billionaire, **George Soros** (opposite), 2004's biggest campaign donor and a big fan of super-restrictive regulations.

OPEN SOCIETY INSTITUTE

GEORGE SOROS

Energy? Who Needs Energy?
If you want a ride, just rent a jet like me.

Net Worth: $8.5 billion (2007, *Forbes*).
Born: August 12, 1930 Budapest, Hungary.
Occupation: investor, philanthropest (not a typo), political activist.
Gave over $23 million to defeat George Bush in 2004.
Engages in currency speculation – deliberately driving national currencies up or down for his personal gain, regardless of how his actions impacted countries, workers and families.
Bankrolls activist groups that oppose economic development, such as revival of mining in Romanian village where 70% of workers are unemployed and families survive on $2 a day. The groups spent millions to stop a mine that would generate thousands of jobs and clean up a 100-year legacy of pollution – but haven't spent one dime on the village or pollution abatement.
Tries to hijack resources of poor counties: In Kosovo, invested $50 million to control the Trepca mine complex worth $5 billion.

Soros and his Open Society Institute recently expended huge amounts of money to support radical pressure groups that are working to prevent poverty-stricken Eastern European countries from approving vital economic development initiatives, such as mining and energy operations. He also supports groups like the Institute for America's Future ($300,000 in 2005), the "incubator" for the Apollo Alliance, which has big plans for energy and economic development here in the United States.

For those who haven't been following the emergence of the Apollo Alliance, Senator Clinton's climate campaign speech may sound like mere rhetoric.

It's actually a virtual quote from a serious political project that's been hatching for more than five years in a new group with an elaborate, detailed script for your entire future.

The group is the Apollo Alliance, a consortium of environmentalists, labor unions, left-leaning civic groups, Democrat governors, and subsidy-seeking new energy businesses.

Apollo's website (www.apolloalliance.org) carries the headline, "Clean Energy and Good Jobs." The basic premise is that we can create millions of good jobs by rebuilding America to be energy efficient while at the same time driving the development of "clean energy" with government money and mandates, which supposedly will give us "three million new jobs," and "freedom from foreign oil."

It's a serious enough proposal that Rep. Jay Inslee (D-WA) introduced the New Apollo Energy Act of 2005, and again in 2007, reflecting most of the group's ideas. The group also held an "Apollo Summit" in 2007 with 160 leaders including Senator Hillary Clinton, who touted her Strategic Energy Fund idea to tax oil company profits to pay for wind and solar.

Apollo's President Jerome Ringo (an African-American, by the way), stated Apollo's mission in these terms: "To challenge each other. To grow beyond our institutional identities. And to build a transformational movement that will build a new energy future and, in the process, will change America forever."

Change a few words and you've got a Democrat campaign speech.

If you want an idea what all that would really look like, look on the opposite page and walk through the graphic of the Apollo Agenda prepared by pro-energy author Ron Arnold for his critical book, *Freezing in the Dark*.

If that doesn't mess up your mind for a while, read it again and make a wild guess what all that would cost, then guess who gets to pay for it – and who gets the cash that will be transferred from poor and middle class consumers to wealthy environmentalists, scientists and corporate CEOs who will promote, justify and build all manner of "green technologies" that will "rapidly" fill the Energy Gap between what we have now and what they promise.

Smart electrical grid
- integrate all sources
- computer control
- regional/local generation
- local power storage
- efficient transmission
- improved distribution
- terrorism-proof
- stable failproof grid
- continual innovation

Air travel
- efficient engines
- biofuel research
- ultralight composite airframes
- offsets in ticket price

Agriculture
- integrated output
- wind and solar
- food, feed, fiber, fuel
- land lease for big wind
- solar to get off the grid
- corn and cellulosic ethanol
- animal waste for biogas methane
- tree growing for carbon sequestering
- steep farmland and food price increases

Emissions cap and trade authorities
- regulator sets emissions limit (cap)
- regulator divides limit into permits
- regulator sells permits up to set limit
- businesses buy permits and then sell them to each other as necessary and possible (trade)
- revenues returned to program

Private investment
- Social Venture Network
- subsidy-seeking funds
- social responsibility funds

Policy-driven finance
- Public bonds for retrofitting
- Public bonds for renewable energy
- State development authorities
- State revolving loan programs
- State pension funds directed to energy projects

Housing
- energy saving construction
- efficient appliances
- jobs-housing linkage fees
- employer assisted housing
- transit-linked mortgages
- zoning exclusions
- urban infill

Retrofit buildings
- commercial, industrial, residential
- energy efficient system upgrades
- heating, lighting, refrigeration, ventilation, elevators, air conditioning replacement

Market development
- geothermal electricity
- solar/photovoltaic
- wind power

Research & Development
- hydrogen fuel cell development
- carbon capture technology
- sequestered coal

Public transportation
- new transit starts
- maintain passenger trains
- regional high-speed rail
- improved roads and bridges

Private transportation
- regulations and mandates
- fuel mileage minimum
- emissions control
- junker buyback and scrap
- hybrid and flexfuel mandates
- alternative fuel vehicle market support

Entertainment and amusement
- energy efficient hotels and parking
- efficient rides and attractions

Workforce
- displacement and retraining
- "Just Transition" payoffs
- green jobs for the disadvantaged
- job quality standards
- apprenticeships

Subsidies:
Manufacturing:
existing federal programs
Manufacturing Extension Partnership
Industrial Technologies Program
Industry of the Future

Self-contained health care
- energy self-sufficient hospitals, emergency rooms, medical offices, hospices, and birthing centers

Federal mandates
- renewable fuel standards
- renewable portfolio standards
- renewable energy tax credits

Open space and wildlands
- forbidding clean energy development on lands Apollo's environmental constituency excludes

"Tip of a very big iceberg: Apollo Alliance agenda exemplars"
Ron Arnold, *Freezing in the Dark: Money, Power, Politics and the Vast Left Wing Conspiracy,*
1st Edition, © 2007 Reproduced with permission of Merril Press

That's what really lies behind the campaign promises.

Senator Clinton claims her plan would cut foreign oil imports by two-thirds, compared with current projections. She doesn't mention that forcing the auto industry to downsize, plasticize and economize cars to double their mileage will cost thousands of dollars per car – and thousands of lives per year, in collisions with buses, trucks, trees, walls and other cars.

She doesn't mention that her plan does nothing to permit greater production of domestic oil and gas and coal from the millions of acres that politicians, judges and environmental activists have placed off limits to drill bits and mine shovels. Under her plan, every barrel of oil saved would be offset by two barrels of lost domestic production.

She doesn't mention that she has no intention of opening even one acre of prime coal deposits that her husband locked up in Utah when he was president – or that, instead, she proposes even more impediments to burning the coal that now generates over half of all the electricity we use. Her plan doesn't even support increased nuclear or hydroelectric power.

Senator Clinton doesn't even mention how all these regulations and wealth transfers will transform your pocket book, your living standards, your job, your transportation, and your dreams for a better tomorrow for yourself and your children.

In a few years, we won't even be running on fumes. We'll be running on perception.

New Mexico Governor Bill Richardson isn't satisfied with an 80% solution. He supports a 90% greenhouse gas reduction by mid-century.

Illinois Senator Barack Obama says climate change is the biggest threat facing black American families today. Not child welfare mothers "raising" illegitimate children in fatherless families. Not substandard, incompetent schools ruled by incivility and violence, and turning out kids who can't read or do math. Not intolerable unemployment levels among black males. Not uneducated youths suited for gangs but not jobs. Climate change.

He claims new technologies will ultimately bring skyrocketing energy costs back down. He didn't say how, or when. He simply insists that, "at least on the front end, there are going to be some costs, and we can't pretend there's a free lunch." That's supposed to be an applause line.

Senator Obama also advocates an odd version of "environmental justice" – the version that the **Sierra Club** (opposite) and several other environmental activist groups devised to stop economic development in poor communities. It holds that even modern facilities, with state-of-the-art pollution controls, might emit some pollution, such as CO_2 – and thus should not be permitted.

SIERRA CLUB

CARL POPE
EXECUTIVE
DIRECTOR

A price-hiking club
With a 770,000 lily-white membership

Hiked energy prices by burying more of your public energy under bureaucratic tombstones than any other environmental lobbyists.
2005 revenue $85 million.
The Sierra Club's mailing list has the highest demographics of any mass group, with more income and education than compassion.
They've got so much lobbying clout and money that they convinced Kansas officials to reject a $3.6 billion coal-fired power plant "to stop global warming" even though it also stopped wind farms that needed the plant's transmission lines – so the state ends up with **no** new energy.
Super-rich hedge fund investor David Gelbaum gave the Sierra Club over $100 million in 2000-2001 in exchange for a promise not to oppose unlimited U.S. immigration, legal and illegal, according to the *Los Angeles Times*. Carl Pope went along with Gelbaum despite the furor it raised within his own monoculture membership, which opposes immigration because more people need more energy and resources.

But when politicians, activists and courts keep businesses out of poor neighborhoods that are already blighted by slum dwellings and brownfields, they take away jobs, health insurance, a stronger tax base for better schools, environmental cleanups, reduced violence, and a chance to own a home and share in the American dream. It leaves permanent welfare as the only option.

With this vision of justice, one has to wonder what our nation's long struggle for civil rights was all about.

Thank goodness American voters have a choice: the Republican candidates.

Republican Senator John McCain of Arizona backs a mere 60% cut in greenhouse gases by 2050.

Former Arkansas governor Mike Huckabee endorses a mandatory carbon cap on everything. He provides no specifics on what his plan is supposed to accomplish.

Virginia Senator John Warner has joined with normally sensible Connecticut Democratic Senator Joe Lieberman to push a "compromise" climate chaos prevention bill that would cut greenhouse gas emissions by "only" two-thirds by that magic "tipping point" year of 2050. Mr. Warner seems to believe this legislation would be a proud legacy for an otherwise undistinguished 20-year Senate tenure.

Former House speaker Newt Gingrich of Georgia has just written a book called *A Contract with the Earth*, touting his bold environmental philosophies. He claims either party could face serious consequences, if it mishandles climate change. A Democrat running on "litigation and regulation" could alienate voters, he said. But Republican candidates who are "anti-environment and deny global warming will get killed in the suburbs."

Apparently, being a leader today – especially being a presidential candidate – means never questioning environmentalist orthodoxy on global warming, fossil fuels, renewable energy or a government-designed-and-mandated future for America's economy and society.

Not even the hefty price tags associated with these questionable solutions to speculative (though loud and insistently proclaimed) problems seems able to generate responsible thinking or robust debate.

Actually, debate is no longer merely avoided.

It's stifled and stigmatized, to silence anyone who raises inconvenient truths about claims being made to promote environmental protection, climate chaos prevention and alternative energy schemes.

Setting out on a path to achieve an 80% reduction in emissions from 1990 levels would cost Americans 30% more for natural gas to heat their homes and even more for electricity, according to expert Tracy Terry, technical director of the National Commission on Energy Policy.

The cost of coal could quadruple, crude oil prices could rise by an extra $24 a barrel, and gasoline prices could go up an additional dollar per gallon or more. And that's just by 2015.

Prices would rise steadily decade after decade – impacting companies, workers, families, retirees, minorities and the poor more and more severely, with every passing year.

One would think that those who most vigorously espouse these claims about the need to banish fossil fuels to avert a climate catastrophe would lead the way via personal sacrifice, or at least lead stay-at-home lives of moderation and energy conservation. One would be wrong.

Al Gore is famous for flying private jets to hundreds of speaking engagements, which net him millions of dollars a year, and having a mansion that consumes 20 times more electricity than the average American home. He refuses to economize and justifies his extravagant fossil use by obtaining "carbon offsets" from groups that claim to reduce global CO2 levels by planting trees and funding clean-energy projects. The former vice president doesn't even buy these carbon offsets with his own money, the way Medieval nobles purchased indulgences from the Catholic Church. He gets them free from his company.

Several Democratic presidential candidates do buy their carbon offset indulgences, however. Mr. Edwards gave $22,000 to NativeEnergy, to atone for the emissions of his campaign's travel – though nothing to cover the energy for his 30-room, 28,000-square-foot mansion. Senator Clinton gave $11,500 to the same group to cover her campaign's operations in April through July 2007. Connecticut Senator Christopher Dodd paid $1,000 to CarbonFund. org for three months of campaigning, and uses a charter air company that claims to offset the carbon footprint of its flights.

Sen. Hillary Clinton started telling Americans to wrap their water heaters in blankets and ditch fluorescent light bulbs, but her jet-setting, two-home lifestyle has some folks wondering if she's maybe being hypocritical.

But, Earth Day Network said it's more important that she introduce "a radical new plan" for energy.

In May 2007, for example, Clinton once traveled in three different private jets in a single day – a Gulfstream II, a Gulfstream III, and a Hawker 800.

A Gulfstream III jet emits 10,078 pounds of carbon dioxide into the air per hour while a Hawker 800 measures up at 4,149 pounds per hour, according to estimates by TerraPass. By comparison, the average American generates only about 15,000 pounds of carbon dioxide in an entire year.

However, Kathleen Rogers, president of the Earth Day Network, told Cybercast News Service that Clinton's proposed energy plan was more important than her personal lifestyle. So is the fact that she is bringing green issues to the political forefront, especially climate change.

"I would love to answer, yes, she's a total hypocrite. But I guess I really don't feel that way," Rogers said. "Do I admire candidates who live [the green lifestyle]? Absolutely.

"But right now, the biggest thing she has to do is come out with a radical new plan that works, that economists can get behind even if it's a hill to climb – and I want to see more, bolder, more creative, more inspiring stuff out of her. And I think we will."

The Apollo Alliance may have dreamed it up first. But it is Senator Clinton and her political allies who will actually implement and impose the Alliance's grand agenda.

Perhaps even more disturbing: To the extent that the tree planting and clean-energy projects are carried out in poor, energy-deprived Third World countries, these "socially responsible" actions have clearly irresponsible consequences. Over two billion people in those countries rarely or never have electricity, and the proposed renewable energy projects can never generate enough electricity to power modern homes, hospitals, offices, shops, factories, schools and societies.

These poor people may eventually get enough juice to power a light bulb and hot plate in their huts, courtesy of a little solar panel on their roofs. But they will remain impoverished – while their kleptocrat leaders pocket substantial sums for helping to "facilitate" these "eco-friendly" programs that make US politicians and movie stars feel less guilty about their profligate lifestyles.

What about these destitute people's civil rights – their right to reliable, affordable electricity, and to choose their own energy and economic futures? Is this what is meant by ecological ethics, environmental justice, climate disaster prevention and sustainable energy on a global scale?

What other costs ought to be considered in the ongoing non-debates about energy and the environment?

To reach the goal of 80% carbon dioxide reduction by 2050, Americans would have to capture and store carbon emissions from every single power plant in the country, notes Edward Parson, a University of Michigan law professor who worked in the Office of Science and Technology Policy under President Bill Clinton. "A world that gets to that big a reduction in greenhouse gases is a world where you're paying more for energy," he said.

A lot more, in fact. These proposed mandates would add hundreds of billions of dollars to the cost of generating electricity and powering, heating and cooling America's factories, offices and homes.

They would add hundreds, or even thousands, of dollars to every family's annual energy and living costs. (Just tell your boss you need a $2000 annual raise.)

And what if the gases escape from one of these high-tech underground CO2 storage reservoirs we hear about? In 1986, a deadly cloud of carbon dioxide erupted so quickly from Lake Nyos in Cameroon that people had no time to react or escape. Over 1700 were asphyxiated.

Amid all their rants about the supposed costs and risks of climate change, have our candidates pondered or addressed *these* costs and risks?

Senator Dodd is the one Democrat to back a straightforward carbon tax on gasoline and other fuels. (That's anathema to most politicians, who prefer to hide the thousand-dollar price tags of their experiments on the American economy, by using cap-and-trade and other schemes.) Dodd has vowed to put the $50 billion he says would be generated annually toward fast-tracking research, development and deployment of renewable power generation and energy efficiency technologies.

Democrats will counter expected GOP attacks on efforts to prevent climate chaos, he says, by making climate policy "part of the economic revival of the country."

(That's the Apollo Alliance agenda talking. Again.)

"We're borrowing a billion a day to bring fuel from offshore," he said – not that he would ever support onshore or offshore domestic drilling to reduce the amount of fuel we bring from offshore sources. As for the costs associated with confronting climate change: "I don't know how you can think that price is as bad as what we're paying right now."

Actually, it's not just the price. It's those alternatives that don't exist. It's trashing people's jobs, family budgets, dreams, retirement savings and civil rights for something that doesn't exist. It's treating them like Guinea pigs, in a massive experiment –

...advocated by environmental groups that seek greater power over your energy, housing, travel and economic decisions, and millions more in grants from foundations and taxpayer-supported government agencies;

...promoted by corporations that seek mandates requiring consumers to purchase energy generated by their new technologies, and by government subsidies to design and build those new technologies;

...supported by scientists who want the $6.5 billion 2007 budget for climate change research continued in perpetuity, and who *negotiate the truth* with United Nations panels like political horse-traders; and

...conducted by politicians and bureaucrats who seek to transform American and world society, based on the assumption that the most terrifying climate disasters conjured up by unverified computer models are actually real.

Who is going to hold all these "guardians of the public welfare" accountable if they are wrong ? And how will we hold them accountable?
Voting them out of office?
Denying them their fat pensions?
Or giving them the Enron treatment: paid vacations in the Big House.

I'm putting them on notice right now:
We refuse to approve your high-priced Apollo Alliance "solutions" to exaggerated environmental problems.
We demand policies that ensure that Americans of every socio-economic status have the abundant, reliable, affordable energy they need, so that they can enjoy in real life the freedoms and opportunities they are guaranteed by our Constitution.
Yes, protect our environment – but not from "inconvenient truths" negotiated in closed-door committees by insatiable grant-seeking scientists.
And don't you "save the world" on the backs of America's poorest.

Politicians justify these destructive plans with scientific logic. But let us not forget that logic without common sense can give us sheer hogwash. The great inventor Charles Kettering knew from vast practical experience:

"Logic is an organized procedure for going wrong with confidence and certainty."

Well, my friends, so is politics.

We need energy reality – not energy illusion.

Keeping politicians honest about energy.
That is the job of the Energy Keepers.

We've all been scared half to death by horror movies – especially by films that are just plausible enough to make us think it could happen.

But when we leave the theater, we know it was just a movie. We might have a few nightmares. But we're not going to buy a million-dollar security system.

Jurassic Park is a perfect example. What if a mosquito bit a tyrannosaurus, and then got fossilized in prehistoric pine resin? And what if scientists extracted DNA from the dinosaur blood, and grew new dinosaurs? And what if some escaped – and started eating people? It would be a disaster!

Thank goodness they were just computer-generated monsters.

Now there's a new genre of horror movies, and a lot of folks want to convince you the terror is *real*. They say we have to spend hundreds of billions of dollars, and drastically curtail our lifestyles – to prevent a climate Armageddon.

What if carbon dioxide from cars, homes, power plants, cows and people caused runaway warming? What if the Earth kept getting hotter and hotter? What if ice caps melted, and seas rose 50 feet, and we had monster hurricanes? It would be a disaster!

Yes, it would be. But before we sacrifice our energy system, economy, living standards and liberties, let's walk out of the theater, and take a deep breath.

Unless I've missed some momentous new scientific evidence, climate disaster claims are just special effects, scary headlines and political hobgoblins. Our planet is not in danger. But your energy and economic civil rights certainly are. Let's look at a few fundamental facts.

Weather and climate change is normal.

If you'll notice, the glaciers that carved the Great Lakes aren't there any more. They vanished suddenly about ten or eleven thousand years ago and left the lakes behind.

So, is global warming real and is it natural? Of course it is.

Then why make a big issue of it?

There's a difference between global warming and *human-caused* global warming. That's where a lot of the politics comes in.

There's a difference between global warming and *catastrophic climate chaos*. That's where the rest of the politics comes in.

The politics centers around controlling people with fear over *human-caused catastrophic climate chaos*. Let's sort that out.

Average Global
Temperature

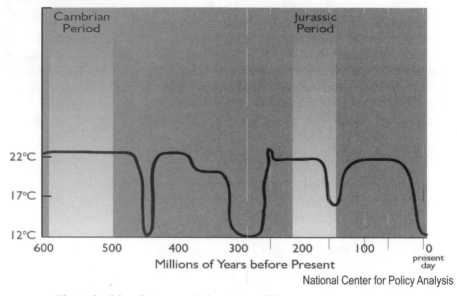

National Center for Policy Analysis

First, the big picture and the 600-million-year long view: When the real Jurassic era dinosaurs roamed the Earth, the average temperature was about 18 degrees F (10 degrees C) warmer than it is today. And look at all those temperature ups and downs in the time chart above.

Climate change has been going on for millions of years. It doesn't mean humans are causing a climate change catastrophe.

In the past few million years, at least four times, mile-thick ice sheets smothered Europe and North America – as hundreds of feet of sea water were converted into massive glaciers. In between, the ice sheets melted, the planet warmed, and seas rose again.

As recently as 5,000 years ago, hippopotami roamed northern Africa, frolicking in lakes, rivers and verdant vegetation. No one really knows why the winds shifted and climate changed, but they did, and the region turned into the Sahara Desert. Beneath its sands you can still find hippo bones, the remains of cities and the outlines of ancient rivers.

A thousand years ago, Vikings raised crops and cattle in Greenland – and it *really was green*. Four centuries later, they were frozen out, Europe was gripped in a Little Ice Age, and priests performed exorcisms on glaciers advancing toward Swiss villages.

There is no evidence that SUVs and coal-fired power plants caused any of this.

The globe finally warmed again from 1850 to 1940. It then cooled for 35 years – then warmed slightly again, by about a half degree Fahrenheit. For the past eight years, average global temperatures have been almost stable: warmer in some places, colder in others, but pretty stable overall.

All these changes in weather, climate, circulation and precipitation patterns affected people, habitats, wildlife and crops. Some benefited, while others were harmed – over and over.

Amid various ups and downs, since 1900 average planetary temperatures rose about one degree F. During that time, our living standards and life expectancies improved dramatically, thanks in large part to fossil fuels. Even if all that warming were due to fossil fuels – a dubious proposition – I'd call it a good trade-off.

Moreover, moderate warming *benefits* agriculture, especially in Canada and Russia. It prolongs growing seasons, and extra carbon dioxide fertilizes plants, helps them grow better, and makes them less susceptible to drought. We can feed more people with less land and water

Wild weather isn't unusual either. Detroit had six snowstorms in April '68, frosts in August '69, a 98-degree heat wave in June '74, and ice-free lakes in January '77. In case you're worried, that was 1868, 1869, 1874 and 1877.

The hottest day on record high for Wisconsin was 114 degrees F, in July 1936. Its record low for a July day was 46 degrees – just five years later, in 1941.

On January 23-24, 1916, Browning, Montana went from +44 to -56 degrees F in 24 hours.

Alaska set a record high of 100 degrees – in 1915 … and a record low of minus 80 in 1971.

Parts of Alaska are in a warming trend right now, as they were in the 1930s. Some scientists say global warming is responsible. Others say it's the Pacific Decadal Oscillation, atmospheric circulation patterns that shift every few decades, bringing warmer or colder air to the Arctic. One such shift occurred about 30 years ago, causing the warming we see now in the Arctic; another took place in the early twentieth century and warmed the region in the 1920s and 1930s.

Actually, in 2007, Arctic sea ice area retreated to its record minimum, as recorded by actual human measurements – which take us back a century or so. However, this minimum is only 4% less than the long-term average for sea ice. And at the same time, Antarctica's sea ice area expanded to its record *maximum*.

So why do so many news stories focus only on the Arctic's latest climate shift – and why do they blame humans? Because crises sell papers.

Pick the right starting point, say 1975, and you see a warming trend. If it continued for 50, 100 or 200 years, the entire Arctic could melt. That's what alarmists are doing now.

But what if you select a different time frame, like 1938 to 1966, when American, Canadian and Russian scientists say Arctic temperatures fell 6 degrees?

At this rate, temperatures would plummet 22 degrees F in one century – and to the equivalent of dry ice (minus 109 F) in just five centuries. That would really affect wildlife and Eskimo culture!

But none of this is likely to happen.

There is no evidence that predominantly human influences have suddenly replaced the natural forces that clearly caused climate and weather cycles in the past: changes in solar energy output, cosmic ray levels, cloud cover, Earth's orbit around the sun, the tilt of Earth's axis, and the turbulent fluids that make up our unpredictable atmosphere and oceans.

There is no evidence that our weather and climate will suddenly be more chaotic because of people – or that people will be unable to adapt to climate changes, the way our far less technologically advanced ancestors certainly did.

In fact, fluctuations in average global temperature correlate better with changes in the sun's radiation than with any rise in CO_2 levels. Actual measurements also suggest that, after a century of high solar activity, the sun's intensity is now declining, and the Earth may soon enter another period of cooling.

Yes, the planet is warming a little, and humans may well be responsible for some of it. But there is no evidence that it's warming any more rapidly than it did last century ... these changes are outside the realm of past (or recent) experience ... Earth may suddenly start warming rapidly or uncontrollably ... or a pattern of unprecedented disasters will suddenly befall us.

Other facts also contradict climate chaos claims.

NASA recently corrected its US temperature records, because of errors in its data. It turns out that the hottest US year on record was not 1998, but 1934. (One reason is that a lot of our temperature stations are right next to air conditioning exhaust vents and other heat sources. No wonder they've been giving off high readings. NASA had to move them and fix its database.)

In fact, five of America's ten hottest years since 1880 were between 1920 and 1940 – and the 15 hottest years since 1880 are spread across seven decades. That sounds like natural variation, not man-made warming.

Half of America endured a month or more of drought in 2002 and 2006. Al Gore and other alarmists say global warming is to blame. But the same thing happened in 1977, 1981 and 1988. And the 1930s Dust Bowl era brought what meteorologists say was the most widespread and ruinous US drought in three centuries. In 1934, almost 80% of the nation was parched by a five-month stretch of virtually no rain.

Ice may be melting along Greenland's edges and in the Western Antarctic Peninsula. But interior Greenland and Antarctica are cooling and gaining ice mass.

Himalayan glaciers are growing, not receding.

Gulf Stream circulation has not slowed.

Even the official 2007 UN climate report says oceans are likely to rise only 12-17 inches over the next century – not 20 feet, as Al Gore claims.

Polar bears are not drowning or endangered. In fact, their populations have doubled since 1970, and they can swim more than 50 miles.

Although the Earth has warmed slightly over the past 30 years, most of this upward trend has taken place in high northern latitudes … in places like Siberia and northern Canada … at night … in the wintertime. From perhaps minus 20 to minus 15 degrees Fahrenheit.

Last I checked, not much ice is going to melt at those temperatures. We're certainly not going to see a wholesale melting of Arctic or Antarctic ice caps.

The graph in Al Gore's movie shows almost no change in average global temperature for a thousand years. Then suddenly, there's a rapid temperature spike, like the blade of a hockey stick. The graph made the Medieval Warm Period disappear, dominated the United Nations' 2001 climate report, and helped persuade several countries to sign the Kyoto climate change treaty.

But then two Canadian researchers showed that the methodology and data were wrong, and the computer algorithm used to generate the hockey stick graph produces the same sudden temperature rise even when totally random numbers are fed into it. The graph was worthless – completely phony.

Mr. Gore still uses the "hockey stick" graph anyway. It's dishonest. But it's effective.

It reminds me of Dr. Stephen Schneider, formerly a global *cooling* alarmist, but now one of the most vocal global warming alarmists. He once told *Discover* magazine, "scientists have to decide what the proper balance is between being effective and being honest."

This is the kind of "honesty," "science" and "scientists" that are driving this runaway "climate disaster prevention" freight train that could send our energy prices into the stratosphere, and ruin our economy and living standards.

Here's maybe the most devastating fact of all.

Former VP Al Gore repeatedly says temperature and carbon dioxide trends have closely paralleled one another for the past 650,000 years. There are "complicating factors," he admits. What factors?

Almost every time, global temperatures rose *first* – and then, several hundred years *later*, carbon dioxide levels increased, as the warmer oceans released their built-up supplies of CO2. Temperatures fell and, centuries later, CO2 levels declined, as cooler oceans absorbed the gas.

Atmospheric CO₂,
parts per million

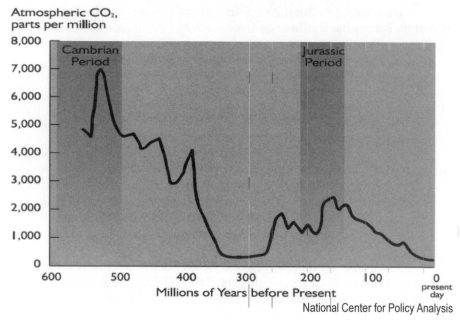

National Center for Policy Analysis

And if we want to take the really long view again, about 500 million years ago in the Cambrian Period, there was an explosion of life forms and CO2 levels were about 18 times what they are today.

During the Jurassic dinosaur period, CO2 levels were as much as 9 times what they are today.

But that business about temperatures rising first and then the CO2 levels following a few hundred years later – that's a huge inconvenient truth! It's the *complete opposite* of catastrophic climate change hypotheses!

It destroys the whole premise for climate chaos prevention laws.

Then what are alarmists relying on to "prove" we face a planetary disaster? Computer models – and worst-case horror movie scenarios generated by the models.

But computer models are not evidence.

Models are assumptions, educated guesses about how things work, in mathematical form. They cannot adequately quantify and analyze our still poor understanding of complex and turbulent climate processes.

They are especially poor at analyzing the effects of water vapor, precipitation and clouds.

They reflect the assumptions that go into them. If the assumptions are wrong, so are the results: garbage in – garbage out. They rarely reflect actual observations of what our climate is doing, and cannot reconstruct past climate patterns, even a year or so ago. They are terrible at predicting future changes, even one year out – much less 10, 50 or 100 years into the future.

They also do a horrible job of projecting regional temperature and precipitation trends. As Dr. John Christy pointed out in testimony before the US Senate in November 2007, one of our top government climate study agencies chose two of the best climate models in the world to describe the future climate for the Southeastern United States. One said it would be jungle-like; the other said it would turn the area into a semi-arid grassland.

(Christy is director of the Earth System Science Center at the University of Alabama in Huntsville and has been a lead author, contributing author or reviewer for every one of the United Nations' climate studies.)

Not a single one of the models that Christy's team examined could reproduce the actual climate of the twentieth century.

Why we should rely on them to predict future climate – and be the primary deciding factor for hundred-billion-dollar energy, economic, housing, transportation, employment and national security decisions – is beyond belief.

A primary reason models don't work is that scientists don't yet understand how precipitation systems and high cirrus clouds work – how they serve as nature's air conditioning system and help regulate temperatures. Most models assume these clouds enhance warming (by providing positive feedbacks that multiply warming effects of CO_2). But recent research by climatologists Christy, Roy Spencer and others suggests that high cirrus clouds may actually have *negative* feedback effects that offset or reduce warming.

Those high clouds trap heat in our atmosphere, and keep it from escaping into outer space. However, when the tropical atmosphere warms, those clouds shrink in coverage, and more escapes – thus *cooling* the planet.

All this helps explain why models cannot forecast much of anything. It is the reason climate scientists don't talk anymore about "predictions" or "projections" or "forecasts." It is the reason climate models use "scenarios" that reflect possible effects of possible human actions, ten or a hundred years from now – to generate hypothetical impacts on climate, crops, coastlines and polar bears.

In other words, modelers are saying: If our worst-case assumptions about future energy use and greenhouse gas emissions are correct ... and if our understanding of oceanic and atmospheric behavior are correct, especially on the ways more CO_2 causes higher temperatures ... and if our models do a decent job of analyzing the data and behavioral changes – then these various (mostly bad) things could happen. So if we plug Assumptions A, B and C into Models Unos, Dos and Tres, then we get these various scenarios.

The problem is, these are very big "ifs," and they are not backed by very good results. In fact, the climate models disagree greatly with each other on the amount of global warming we are likely to see in polar and other regions, and on how and where precipitation patterns are likely to change.

The main thing they agree on is warming in mid-range atmospheric regions of the tropics (the troposphere). Ironically, the models that agree most closely with actual observed data project the least global warming! That's not a very convenient truth, if you're an alarmist.

Still, a lot of computer scenarios are pretty reasonable. But "reasonable" doesn't sell newspapers – or persuade people to give up their energy and economic civil rights.

So alarmists ignore the 2, 3 and 4 degree warming scenarios – and hype the scariest ones. The ones that predict *10 degrees* of *catastrophic* warming, and horrendous floods, droughts, famines, storms and other cataclysms.

Next they put the biggest disaster scenarios together – in a kind of climate chaos pyramid scheme: the worst temperature increases, the worst droughts, the worst floods, the worst ice cap meltdowns, the highest sea level rise, the biggest crop failures. Then they issue press releases – which of course the news media and politicians trumpet, just in time for the next climate negotiations that will determine your future energy and economic civil rights.

That's not science. It's *political* science, Hollywood special effects and fear-mongering.

No wonder there is no consensus.

A lot of scientists still believe in man-made climate disaster. But thousands do not.

Most agree the Earth is warming. They even agree that human pollution and land use changes influence weather patterns and even climate – a little. But there is a huge debate about the causes and effects of warming, and how much warming we can expect, before it starts cooling again.

Very few meteorologists and climatologists say we're heading for a disaster.

A 2003 international survey of 500 climate experts, by German scientists Dennis Bray and Hans von Storch, found that:

- A third disagree that recent climate change is mostly due to man-made causes.
- Two-thirds do not agree that we know enough to reasonably assess the effects of greenhouse gases.
- Over half say we cannot make "reasonable predictions" of climate variability even one decade into the future.
- Most say warmer temperatures would have both beneficial and harmful effects. Some people, places, plants and wildlife would be harmed, but others would benefit.

In addition to that survey, more than 18,000 scientists have signed the Oregon Petition, which says there is "no convincing evidence" that greenhouse gas emissions are causing "catastrophic heating of the Earth's atmosphere and disruption of the Earth's climate." Other scientists have signed similar documents, saying no disaster is imminent or likely.

Then where do the consensus claims come from? It's a classic "bait and switch," given credence by constant repetition, and promoted by those who see "climate change disaster" as the most ingenious claim yet devised to put control over our "master resource" in the hands of professional alarmists, politicians and bureaucrats.

If most scientists agree that Earth has warmed ... and humans played a role in this warming ... and temperatures could continue rising ... and some effects of continued warming are likely to be harmful – then there must be a consensus that there has been unprecedented global warming, humans are responsible, we are reaching a "tipping point," temperatures will soar anther 10 degrees F, and we are heading for a planetary catastrophe.

Bait and switch tactics are illegal in consumer sales. They ought to be illegal in political sales, as well.

Here's another point to keep in mind.

We've been down this path before.
Catastrophic global warming is just the latest in a long line of gloom and doom predictions by professional alarmists.

The Alar scare bankrupted a lot of family orchards – but channeled millions of dollars into environmentalist coffers. The dioxin scare closed a Missouri town – but got the chemical banned.

Scare stories that Environmental Defense and other radical groups promoted about DDT took it out of the public health arena. Millions of African women and children died from malaria, who would likely have lived if their countries had been able to spray the walls of their houses to keep disease-carrying mosquitoes from coming in.

Not once have those alarmists apologized – or been held accountable. Now many of the same groups are promoting the biggest ecological scare of all time.

The economic, disease and death tolls never bothered them. Do you honestly believe they will be troubled by the impacts their energy and climate "solutions" will have on you?

It's bad enough that their climate chaos "solutions" would scrap our energy system, trash our economy, send our jobs overseas, to countries that have no CO_2 rules, and give unaccountable activists, politicians and bureaucrats power over every aspect of our lives. Our reliance on fossil fuels is so great that the massive greenhouse gas cutbacks they routinely toss around would have disastrous consequences, especially for minorities.

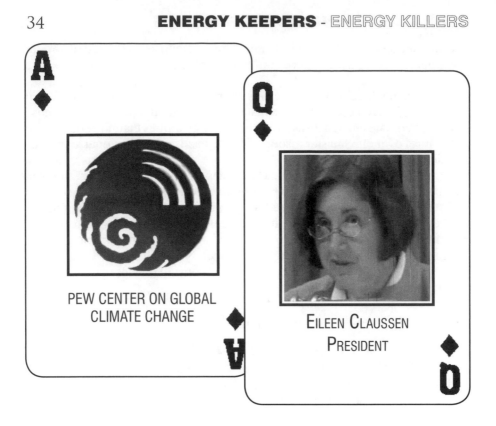

A
◆

PEW CENTER ON GLOBAL
CLIMATE CHANGE   ◆

Q
◆

Eileen Claussen
President   ◆

Oil money against oil needs
Pew oil money against your oil needs

Real Name: Strategies for the Global Environment doing business as Pew Center on Global Climate Change.

Recruits businesses to seek government subsidies for non-fossil energy sources and oppose fossil fuels.

2006 income: $3.7 million; Pew Trusts gave $21 million (2000-2003).

Claussen salary: $298,502; benefits $20,895.

Established 1998 by the Pew Charitable Trusts (7 trusts, created by the wealth of **Sun Oil Company** founder, Joseph Newton Pew).

Pew's investment portfolio is still built on shares of the very industries it's trying to undermine – fossil fuels: According to the IRS, J.N. Pew Jr. Trust owns millions worth of shares in ExxonMobil, Chevron, ConocoPhillips, Anadarko, Valero Energy, and many others. Pew uses its vast oil wealth to deny you access to your publicly-owned energy, drive up the price of oil, gas and electricity, and force you to depend on expensive, unreliable wind and solar energy.

Even worse, these sacrifices by countless American families would reduce average global temperatures by maybe 0.05 degrees. We can't even measure that. In fact, US government atmospheric scientists say, even perfect compliance with the global-economy-wrecking Kyoto Protocol would reduce temperatures by just 0.2 degrees.

But there will be no "perfect compliance." For all their moral preening and criticism of the United States, only one Western European country (Sweden) is likely to meet its Kyoto emission goals. China, India and other developing countries are building cars and fossil-fuel power plants at a feverish pace – and they aren't required to abide by Kyoto at all.

So no matter what we do, no matter how much we cripple our economy, in the name of preventing catastrophic climate change – all our sacrifices would be for nothing.

Perhaps worst of all, this pain would be on top of the new taxes, tax hikes and layers of new regulations that Congress and states are imposing on us, year after year. The only ones to profit will be the corporations that cash in on new government subsidies as promoted by the **Pew Center on Global Climate Change** (profile opposite). Poor and minority families especially will pay a terrible price – for no environmental gain.

And yet, Senator Barbara Boxer insists on saying global warming is equivalent to "leaving a child alone in a hot, locked car." As chairman of the Senate Environment and Public Works Committee, she is determined to enact punitive legislation to "prevent climate chaos."

Her favorite seems to be the Lieberman-Warner bill. It would require companies and America to slash carbon dioxide emissions to 1990 levels by 2020 – and 65% *below* 1990 levels by 2050. To gauge how disastrous these draconian measures are, ponder the following.

Beware of the coming economy-killing climate juggernaut.

The United States emitted 5 billion metric tons of CO_2 in 1990. In 2006, we emitted almost 6 billion tons. If Lieberman-Warner becomes law, we would have to wipe out one-sixth of our 2006 emissions in twelve years – and a whopping 70% of emissions by 2050. And that assumes we just freeze our emissions, population, energy use, economic growth and employment opportunities at 2006 levels for the next 42 years. Whom are they trying to kid?

Unless we have a massive, immediate shift to nuclear and hydro-electric power, there is no way this can possibly be done, short of a national economic suicide pact and the destruction of our energy and economic civil rights.

Actually, even this won't help. According to the UN's 2007 Fourth Assessment Report, even having 1,000 huge new nuclear power plants fully operational by 2020 would result in Earth's average temperature being only 0.3 degrees F cooler by 2100, than if we did nothing.

But Senators Boxer, Lieberman, Warner and Obama have said nothing to suggest that they plan to promote nuclear or hydroelectric. Their "solution" is to mandate conservation and renewable energy. They'll just require that we decimate our energy use, and expand our wind and solar power from 0.4% of our energy today – to some 80% of it in just 40 years.

That certainly sounds achievable. All Congress has do is *pass a law requiring* that it happen. While they're at it, they could pass a law mandating that all Americans have IQs of 160 and no more than 2% body fat by 2050. That would do the trick. We're a nation of laws, after all.

It's time for a reality check.

Various analysts have calculated that this "Climate Security Act" would cost our nation tens of billions of dollars a year – hundreds of billions a decade. Senator Joe Lieberman himself has conceded that his bill would cost the United States "hundreds of billions of dollars." The cost of buying food and clothing, driving our cars, heating our homes and keeping workers employed will soar.

CRA International (Charles River Associates) estimates that it would cost us *$4 trillion* to *$6 trillion* over 40 years! That's a drop in average household purchasing power of $1700 to $2500 per year, for every family of four in America. Combined business investment would fall by $200 billion. The cost of petroleum products would more than double.

These kinds of budgetary body blows may not hurt upper-crust Hollywood or Cape Cod households. But for average minority families, every dollar that legislators force them to spend on "preventing climate change" will be one less dollar they have to drive their cars, heat and cool their homes, buy food, pay for medical care, take a vacation, pay for college and retirement, and run their small business. Moreover, every one of these items will also cost more – which means the economic impact would be even worse.

Your politicians apparently think you have nothing better to spend your hard-earned paychecks on than speculative ecological catastrophes, conjured up by activists, headlines and computers. They're apparently willing to leave you freezing jobless in the dark.

Of course, they deny that. They promise their "energy revolution" will help America achieve a "cleaner, more secure energy future, stay competitive and strong, create good jobs and build a cleaner, safer world," as Minnesota Governor Tim Pawlenty intoned when he unveiled the previously hush-hush Midwestern Governors climate change pact in November 2007.

The agreement sets emission targets that are "consistent with" the 60-80% reductions demanded by the United Nations' Intergovernmental Panel on Climate Change.

The new rules will require expensive CO_2 removal, transportation and storage, "advanced" bio-fuels, "thousands of new megawatts of wind energy," and "cost-effective, sustainable, environmentally responsible energy."

If only their hot air could be harnessed to generate electricity.

There's an alternative. We could keep our economy humming along … continue developing newer, better energy technologies and pollution controls … and adapt to any climate changes that occur – the same way our ancestors did, thousands of years ago, hundreds of years ago, during the Dust Bowl, and countless other times.

And those climate changes will come, no matter what we do to re-create Camelot, when King Arthur was able to sing: "It's true. It's true. The Crown has made it clear. The climate must be perfect all year."

Adaptation would be far less expensive, and can be targeted to where it is needed most, to the most pressing societal and ecological problems, without all the undesirable consequences of massive catastrophic climate change "solutions."

That's the approach advocated by Danish environmentalist Bjorn Lomborg. He believes humans are helping to cause climate change, but he doesn't believe in spending hundreds of billions of dollars on solutions that won't work … will cause devastating harm to poor and middle class families … and will effectively prevent us from having enough money to address critical problems that we can (and must) do something about.

We can't afford to fix our aging schools, bridges, roads and transmission lines. We can't afford to spend more than $2 billion a year, helping to eradicate malaria in Africa. We can't afford to solve HIV/AIDS, tuberculosis and other diseases of poverty.

But somehow we can afford to spend hundreds of billions of dollars to stop a climate change monster conjured up by computer models, alarmists and headline writers? How is *that*?

Meanwhile, in a dozen other countries …
While you're pondering how all this is going to affect you – and how much all your pain is going to prevent "runaway global warming," don't forget China, India, Brazil, Indonesia and other rapidly growing economies. They are not required to do any of this.

China is now the world's biggest source of man-made carbon dioxide, and Chinese CO_2 emissions are projected to more than double between 2004 and 2030, the US Chamber of Commerce calculates. Other analysts say carbon dioxide emissions from China's power plants will rise some 60% over just the next decade.

India's emissions will go up 130% over the next 25 years. Europe's will continue rising, as well – not only in Eastern Europe, which is playing catch-up after decades of oppressive rule and stagnant economic growth – but also in Western Europe. By 2050, developing country emissions could account for 70-80% of all global CO_2 emissions, according to experts.

Alarmists in eco groups, the UN and the International Energy Agency insist that average global temperatures will rise to "a devastating level" by 2030 if China and India do not begin curbing energy use and carbon emissions immediately.

But of course this hysteria too is based on models, ideology and an intense desire to put international government agencies in charge of people's energy and economic decisions. It is not based on science, or on any rational projections of temperature and climate that reflect observed temperature data or an analysis of solar energy trends as a primary cause of climate change.

We can pressure these countries all we want with environmental, economic and moral arguments. We can offer to give them our best energy production, pollution reduction, electricity generation and manufacturing technologies – thereby sending even more American jobs overseas, as *they* become more productive and competitive, while *we* become less so.

But they are still not going to end the New Industrial Revolution that is lifting their people out of poverty. And that revolution requires energy – primarily fossil fuel energy. They can't afford to stop their fast-paced development. They'd have a very different kind of revolution on their hands, if they did.

There's a lot of talk about "environmental justice." But the real environmental injustice is the way pressure groups, bureaucrats and politicians are using climate scares to prevent energy development in impoverished countries. In Africa, almost *600 million people* rarely or never have electricity. In many parts of Asia and Latin America, the deprivation is just as bad.

This unbelievable energy deprivation prolongs indescribable poverty, disease and death that could be reduced if countries had abundant, reliable, affordable energy: to build their economies – and to stop having to use wood and dung for heating and cooking fires that cause indoor air pollution and millions of deaths from lung diseases every year.

But these nations are being told climate change is the gravest threat they face. They are being told their future must be restricted to "safe renewable energy." And if that energy isn't really available for a few more decades, they'll just have to wait.

So if the Third World doesn't "do as it's told" on climate change, and the world still has to reduce global CO2 emissions by 60-80% to avert this supposed climate cataclysm – then what? Then the "responsible" developed countries will have to slash their emissions by some 95% over the next few decades. How will your family and community do that?

And what guarantee do you have that these economy-killing energy reductions and CO2 removals will affect global climate change by more than a few tenths of one degree?

And if all these hysterical alarmists are wrong – and you lose your job, your home, your retirement nest egg, all the gains minority America made since ratification of the Fourteenth Amendment – then what?

Or what if they bury all that CO2, at a cost of hundreds of billions of dollars – but some escapes, and thousands of people get asphyxiated? What then?

Then you get to vote against re-electing the politicians. And you get to say nasty things about the bureaucrats, pressure groups and corporate rent-seekers that created, promoted and railroaded these ideas into law.

That's about all the accountability they'll be subject to. But what if an enraged populace returns us to the days of Frontier Justice, when citizens had no other recourse to protect their families? That is a terrible worry.

But no one has even taken the time to ponder any of this.

The climate change prevention juggernaut is moving too fast for that.

Right here in America, Lieberman-Warner, the Midwestern Governors' pact, and their assorted climate chaos prevention clones are moving full speed ahead. They are likely to bring incalculable personal, economic and family pain ... unprecedented control of our lives by unaccountable bureaucrats ... the loss of basic freedoms and civil rights ... and living standards akin to what our ancestors endured decades ago – for no detectable planetary carbon dioxide reduction, and certainly no detectable environmental gain or climate stabilization.

Have our politicians completely lost their marbles?

Even worse, millions of Americans seem convinced that these global warming Frankenstein monsters are real. They seem to be prepared to accept the pain, unemployment, reduced living standards and lost freedoms.

They're willing to buy into the notion that covering an area twice the size of Virginia with gigantic wind turbines, to produce unreliable "eco-friendly" electricity from "free" renewable wind power – and planting an area twice the size of Indiana in corn, to produce "sustainable" ethanol – is preferable to drilling for oil and gas in Alaska and our western states or on our Outer Continental Shelf. And preferable to burning coal or building new nuclear power plants.

Have we also completely lost our marbles?

Who's going to get hurt worst of all by all this insanity? The poor, the elderly, others on fixed incomes. Minorities, most of all.

Every extra dollar they are forced to pay for energy is a dollar they won't have for other "luxuries," such as tuna and noodle casseroles, paying the mortgage they just refinanced to reduce their payments and get another loan to live on, saving for retirement on dog food in a cold house, buying clothing from the Salvation Army, sending kids to the local community college, patching a roof that desperately needs to be replaced, taking a well-deserved vacation at the local Motel 6, and purchasing retread tires for the clunker they can't afford to trade in.

Over 45 million Americans have fixed incomes and depend on Social Security checks, 60 Plus Association president Jim Martin told Congress in May 2007. When energy prices increase, seniors pay disproportionately more, because so many are on fixed incomes.

"To keep up with energy costs, must they cut back on groceries?" he asked. "On prescription drugs? On doctor visits?"

A November 2007 Pew Research Center survey found that 43% of US blacks say the black-white economic gap has widened. Under any of these climate bills, that situation can only get worse.

Senator Obama insists that catastrophic climate change is the greatest threat facing black America today. If he means the proposed government *response* to this phony crisis, he's right. Otherwise I'd like to know what he's smoking.

What can you expect in life under the new Climate Czars? My guess is that it will be akin to what British citizens might have to endure, under newly proposed greenhouse gas emission rules. According to the London *Daily Mail*, the rules envision a new carbon trading scheme for local city councils, supermarkets and large retail outlets.

They could well result in personal carbon quotas, under which every citizen is given a fixed amount of carbon to use every year. Everyone's consumption and carbon use would be monitored, and frugal people could sell their spare rations to those who want to want to indulge a little. Those who exceed their carbon allowance could be barred from flying or driving.

The new rules could also result in green taxes on a host of consumer items; sharply higher fuel prices, in a nation that already pays almost twice what we do; and higher commuter fees, already at $16 a day, for the privilege of driving in London.

Supporters say the rules are needed to save the planet. Critics say the restrictions would result in increased economic slowdowns, factory closings and job losses across the country – and more people leaving Britain, which is already losing 1,000 fed-up citizens a day – for scant environmental gain.

The monetary total for all of this? Just in Britain, at least $20 billion per year for the next 42 years, which does not include the costs of building "greener" power stations, creating better public transport systems, closing polluting factories, or the brain and labor drain of young people voicing their displeasure with their feet.

I presume the Brits can put the hefty tab on their Mastercards.

The total in lost personal freedom? Priceless.

Britain has a duty to lead by example, a government spokesman insisted – even if China and India continue building cars and coal-fired power plants, and all the sacrifices bring no environmental benefit. Many citizens are in a rebellious mood.

The actions are "desperately needed," Friends of the Earth director Tony Juniper responded. In fact, "the Government must strengthen its proposals to make them truly effective." The French equivalent of which is "Let them eat cake."

Speaking of France, Reuters reports that more than 70 Gallic towns have already replaced petroleum-powered municipal vehicles with "eco-friendly" horse-drawn carriages that cost about $17,000 and feature disk brakes, signal lamps and removable seats.

"It's all about sustainable development and bringing some humanity back to today's monotonous, machine-driven jobs," a proponent said. He predicted that many more communities would do likewise.

Sustainable? Eco-friendly? Climate-friendly? Especially on a global scale?

Has anyone calculated how many millions of acres would have to be planted in forage, to feed all the pretty horses – and how much water, fertilizer, insecticide and fuel it would take to grow that forage?

Has anyone figured out how much manure they would drop on city streets? Back in 1900, New York City alone had to dispose of some *90,000 tons* of horse manure annually, along with millions of gallons of horse urine.

Most just went into local rivers. The rest simply added to the city's aromatic ambience, and got pounded into fine dust, contributing greatly to the endemic tuberculosis problem. Can you imagine the environmental effects of New York and other major cities switching to horse-drawn taxis, delivery trucks, and government and personal cars?

Back to the future, indeed.

Well, this won't happen here, you say. Really?

The US Supreme Court has already decreed that the same carbon dioxide you exhale thousands of times a day is a "pollutant" that threatens our planet. A three-judge federal appeals court in California has decreed that new fuel-economy standards for light trucks and sport utility vehicles are not tough enough, because regulators didn't thoroughly assess the impact of tailpipe emissions that contribute to climate change.

The Midwestern Governors Association is pushing ahead with its plans. So is Congress.

Are you ready to bet your house, predicting where this will end?

It may well be that a couple hundred countries have signed the Kyoto Protocol on climate change, which the US still has not ratified. Signing such a treaty is one thing. Enforcing it – at great economic cost and pain – is another.

Most of these countries can sign any treaty they want. For them, the treaties are mostly symbolic. If the pain becomes too unbearable, or too many people complain too much, the requirement to slash emissions to 7% below 1990 levels can simply be ignored. That's what's happening in the European Union, where several countries are well above their agreed emission limits.

But in the United States, once we sign a treaty, it becomes the Law of the Land. It gets enforced, by regulations and courts. And if it's not enforced to the satisfaction of various aggrieved parties and pressure groups, they go to court and make sure it's followed to the letter – and your job, salary, budget, mortgage payment, heating and cooling bills, medical bills and civil rights are not going influence the final judicial decree.

Ditto for any "climate protection" laws that Congress enacts.

Now, it may be that we humans really are affecting Earth's climate to a profound degree, and we are heading for a climate disaster – at least for some parts of the planet.

But before I make huge personal sacrifices, and surrender my energy and economic civil rights ... before I ask you to do so – I want real, demonstrable, replicable, scientific evidence – the same kind I needed when I was studying chemistry in college and working in the medical field. The same kind that pharmaceutical companies have to provide, under carefully monitored independent studies, before they put a new drug on the market.

I want proof that we are heading for a climate disaster, and humans are to blame, and the "solutions" are actually going to stabilize a climate that has never been stable, and never will be.

I'm not going to settle for a bunch of headlines, hype, hysteria, computer models, worst-case scenarios and global warming horror movies.

But I am going to temper my fears about catastrophic global warming with my clear memories of the catastrophic global cooling fear campaign just a few decades ago – caused, of course, by the burning of fossil fuels. A University of California-Davis professor told a 1970 Earth Day crowd, "If present trends continue, the world will be ... 11 degrees colder by 2000," which is "twice what it would take to put us in an ice age."

The *Christian Science Monitor* observed that the cold had driven armadillos out of Nebraska, glaciers were advancing and "growing seasons had shortened around the world." A 1975 *Newsweek* article claimed meteorologists were "almost unanimous" in their concern that a major "cooling trend" would "reduce agricultural productivity for the rest of the century," possibly leading to "catastrophic" famines.

International Wildlife warned that "a new ice age must now stand alongside nuclear war" as a true threat to mankind. The *New York Times*, *Washington Post* and many others waded in with additional worries about global cooling and "evidence" of "profound changes" that would wreak havoc on our planet.

Where the catastrophic climate change industry is concerned, good memories and a healthy dash of skepticism help keep things in perspective.

Where family budgets and living standards are concerned, what might help keep climate change concerns in perspective is the simple reality that we need *all* our energy resources, unless we're prepared to send our economy, health and living standards back somewhere along the path toward what our grandparents and great grandparents "enjoyed" a century ago.

Our population is growing. Our energy needs are expanding. And we need the coal, oil and gas resources that activists, politicians and courts are regulating or pricing out of reach for millions of Americans.

For those who are concerned about climate change, the potential for wind and solar is very limited, in the opinion of most experts – but nuclear power is a greenhouse-gas-free energy source that promises to grow in importance.

Nuclear power plants eliminated the release of 691 million tons of carbon dioxide that would have been emitted in 2006 if their electricity had come from coal, oil or natural gas, according to the Environmental Protection Agency. That's equal to the carbon dioxide released from nearly all US passenger cars.

Nuclear generates 20% of America's electricity and plays an essential role in meeting our nation's growing demand for more vital electrical power. Nuclear plants provide large amounts of reliable, low-cost electricity, offer stable long-term prices, and have a relatively small environmental impact or land use footprint, especially compared to wind and solar.

As our largest and only expandable source of emission-free electricity, nuclear energy is essential to America's economic and environmental future. It can withstand extreme weather and climate conditions and produces electricity around the clock, with a 90% capacity or reliability factor. Facilities are well protected against terrorist attacks, and storage of wastes is more a political than a safety or environmental problem.

The fuel for nuclear power plants is abundant, represents a small portion of the generation costs, and comes from trusted allies like Canada and Australia. These factors make future prices of nuclear- generated electricity both predictable and affordable, and new standardized plant designs (including "pebble bed reactors) will further improve safety, construction times and price considerations.

So once again, it's a matter of choices and tradeoffs.

But we need the energy.

The future is largely up to you. Will you be an Energy Keeper? A Civil Rights Keeper?

Or will you just let Energy Killers consign you to the energy ghetto?

CHAPTER 4

RENEWABLE FANTASIES

If catastrophic climate change is the fear factor driving many environmental agendas and policies today, renewable energy is the most important element of hope and optimism.

It would be fantastic if our current energy system could be replaced by affordable, reliable, perpetual energy, with no unwanted consequences. That dream is driving investment and research – and countless legislative initiatives – all over the world.

But renewable energy is fantastic in another way, as well. Regardless of the accolades they routinely receive, it is sheer fantasy that we can survive and thrive on non-fossil-fuel technologies any time soon – or that renewable energy technologies will come without serious ecological downsides. We must guard against exaggerated expectations, honestly assess costs and benefits – and make sure we don't trash any part of our existing energy infrastructure, before we truly can replace it with fuels and systems that now are found mostly on drawing boards or in dreams, legislative pronouncements or demonstration projects.

There is such a thing as renewable energy, of course. It already plays an important role in our energy mix – a 7% solution, as the table on page 3 points out. Some technologies fuel homes and industrial processes directly; others generate electricity that is more expensive than the fossil or nuclear variety, but still a welcome addition to power grids. Nearly everyone expects that they will be more prevalent in the future.

However, ad campaigns, public policy decisions and taxpayer outlays need to reflect more hard reality, and less romanticism, hype and even deception. And the fear and loathing that some have for oil, natural gas, coal and nuclear power is no excuse for us, our policy makers or our courts to ignore Energy Reality and widen our Energy Gap, by promoting renewable illusions and closing off access to the real energy we need.

Renewables today – and the promise for tomorrow

Hydroelectric power is the best known and most obvious renewable resource in America. Dams and the turbines inside them, small and large, generate 3% of all the energy we use, and 42% of all the energy that comes from our renewable portfolio.

Built to harness the power of fast-flowing rivers, or to create vast reservoirs along other waterways, hydro projects electrified much of America, especially in the Tennessee Valley, Pacific Northwest and several Southwestern states. Their reservoirs created new habitats for fish and wildlife, launched new opportunities for boating and swimming, and provided water for communities and farmlands.

Except during extensive droughts, hydro power has been a reliable, relatively inexpensive source of energy for millions. It produces no greenhouse gases or other air pollutants. Silt buildup behind dams has mostly been a manageable problem and, while conflicts over water rights for people, farms and wildlife continue, courts and interstate compacts have resolved most of them.

Fortunately or unfortunately, depending on your perspective, we've already built hydroelectric dams on most of the US waterways that could support them. A few dams have already been taken down, to facilitate fish migration, and some environmentalists want other existing facilities removed. The lack of realistic alternatives for replacing that electricity, as well as demand for the water storage and recreation they provide, makes large-scale removal unlikely.

Biomass is the USA's most important renewable resource. Over 48% of all renewable energy comes from trees and other plant matter. The term embraces wood-burning stoves and fireplaces, as well as sawmill wastes that aren't turned into particle board. The biggest component is flammable liquors that paper mills create during the pulp-making process and burn to save on other forms of energy.

These fuels are far less efficient energy sources, because their carbon-to-hydrogen ratios are high (compared to oil, natural gas and even coal), but they utilize resources that otherwise would be discarded and wasted. They also generate particulate, hydrocarbon and CO_2 emissions, though most are controlled with modern "scrubbers" and other technologies.

Perhaps the most recognizable biomass fuel is ethanol. Refined from corn in much the same way we distill grain into whiskey, it has been touted as a way to reduce US dependence on foreign oil, cut greenhouse gas emissions and help farmers. Bolstered by a 51-cent-per-gallon tax credit and protected from foreign competition by a 54-cent-per-gallon import tariff, US producers grew, processed, distilled and transported 5 billion gallons of corn-based ethanol in 2005 ... and 7 billion gallons in 2007.

A fascinating, but little known, biomass program involves waste-to-energy facilities that turn household, office and industrial garbage into electricity. They improve recycling rates, by recovering even paper clips and the metal and glass in products like light bulbs and steel-and-cardboard juice canisters. They also minimize what ends up in landfills – mostly ash that can't be recycled into something else.

The United States generates some 250 million tons of trash a year. Over 40 million tons get burned in about 120 WTE plants that generate nearly 3,000 megawatts of electricity (MWe) – enough for 2.5 million homes.

Wind power hearkens back to pharaoh's barges, clipper ships and Holland's picturesque windmills. Today, enormous high-tech towers – in small clusters or sprawling "wind farms" – generate increasing amounts of electricity that powers homes and other facilities directly or is fed into power grids in virtually every state.

In 2005, wind turbines generated enough electricity to meet the needs of 1.6 million US homes – but the United States still gets only about 0.5% of its total electricity from this source. This sounds trivial compared to Denmark, which gets 20% of its electricity from wind, but America's wind power is actually four times as much as the Danish output, in megawatts per year. The US wind energy component is growing steadily, especially in Texas and California, due to tax breaks, direct government subsidies and legislative mandates that specify percentages of power that must come from renewable sources. Total US wind energy capacity grew by nearly 3,000 MW in 2007, according to the US Energy Information Administration.

The biggest advantage for onshore, nearshore and offshore wind turbines is that their energy can be significant and they generate no greenhouse gases or other emissions. Improved electrical grid equipment makes it easier for companies to integrate wind energy into grids.

The biggest engineering problem involves the fact that wind speed can vary from zero to gale force. At either extreme, electrical output vanishes: no wind means the turbine blades don't turn at all, and the system must be shut down in high winds, to prevent catastrophic accidents. That means a well-sited turbine's actual productivity during a year is only about 35% – the electricity it actually produces compared to what it could if the wind blew constantly at speeds necessary to generate electricity. By comparison, nuclear power plants typically achieve a 90% capacity factor, as they can run pretty much all the time.

Solar energy is generated as either thermal (heat) or photovoltaic (electricity) power. Because it requires open land areas and abundant sunlight, solar power make the most sense in desert-like regions, such as California and the Southwestern United States. However, it has practical applications in many other places, too. Subsidies and tax breaks for installing systems increase their attraction for homeowners and others.

Household thermal systems simply use the sun's energy to heat the home or tanks of water. Industrial thermal systems use curved mirrors to concentrate heat, boil water to make steam, and turn turbine blades that generate electricity. The biggest one ever built is in California's Mojave Desert; it generates 80 MWe – enough for about 67,000 average US homes. (The largest photovoltaic installation to date produces only 12 megawatts.) The Nevada Solar One installation cooks oil, which flows to an adjacent power plant, where it converts water into steam that runs a turbine, in a continuous loop system.

Photovoltaic panels use the sun's photons to move electrons and produce electrical current. Their price has dropped from $22 per watt of capacity in 1980 to around $2-3 per watt in 2006, but the cost of electricity is still very high compared to fossil, nuclear or hydroelectric. Researchers are steadily cutting these costs, by boosting factory and machine productivity, increasing solar cell efficiencies – and using less silicon, by cooling crystalline silicon ingots more slowly and carefully, to boost quality and reduce waste, and cutting thinner slices. Other firms are pursuing thin-film solar power, replacing silicon-based panels with sheets of photovoltaic film made from various less expensive materials.

Geothermal energy is simply the utilization of heat from beneath the Earth's surface, to heat water or buildings, or generate electricity. The Roman spa in Bath, England was fed by hot springs, as are the natural outdoor hot tubs near Aspen, Colorado – and Iceland is famous for its use of power from the volcanic formations beneath the island nation. In Canada, 30,000 small installations provide heat for residences and commercial buildings. Although the total amounts to only 0.3% of all the energy we use, the United States produces more geothermal power than any other nation. Surprisingly, the largest single US producer is an oil company – Chevron.

The most common geothermal systems employ "flash steam," derived from hot water (above 360 degrees F) pumped from high-pressure underground reservoirs. As the water enters the power plant, it "flashes" into steam that drives turbines. Binary-cycle power plants use somewhat cooler water to transfer heat to pipes containing liquids with lower boiling points than water; those liquids then vaporize to operate the turbines. Enhanced or hot-rock geothermal systems pump water into hot formations deep in the Earth, rather than bringing up hot water from tectonically active regions. Hot-rock technology can thus be used almost anywhere.

Energy harnessed from geothermal systems is clean, non-polluting and sustainable, since the water can be re-injected into the ground to produce more steam. Power production is year-round and price-competitive, and facilities can be scaled to power buildings, villages or cities. However, if a power plant uses more heat than the source generates, it can deplete much of the geothermal energy, at least temporarily. In the USA, the best resources tend to be near protected areas – like Yellowstone, Lassen and Hawaii Volcanoes National Parks – and many people fear development will harm the areas' scenic wonders or their geysers and hot springs.

Intelligent building design and basic energy conservation are truly renewable, beneficial and even profitable practices. Turning lights off when you leave a room, substituting LEDs for incandescent bulbs, setting your thermostat lower in winter and higher in summer, and sequencing lights to keep traffic moving, thereby reducing fuel consumption and pollution, are but a few of the things we could all do much more. One could even make a case for eliminating toll booths along interstate highways. The gasoline wasted and pollution emitted by cars waiting to get to booths or EZPass lanes is monumental – and any revenues collected are offset by wages and taxes lost because workers are forced to wait seemingly forever in rush hour traffic.

It has even been suggested that we turn off the air-conditioning in Congress and federal office buildings. This would save energy and cut greenhouse gas emissions. By reducing legislative and bureaucratic activity during hot summer months, it would also ensure that government focuses on high-priority items, rather than enacting more unnecessary rules that burden taxpayers and small businesses.

The realities – economic, technological and ecological

As the late economist Milton Friedman was fond of saying, there is no such thing as a free lunch. As with fossil fuels, all these renewable energy alternatives involve trade-offs: slightly more energy, but at the price of lower affordability and reliability, coupled with more air pollution, larger amounts of materials to build the energy-production facilities, and impacts on aesthetics, cropland and wildlife habitats, to name a few.

There is also the matter of costs, in the form of tax breaks and subsidies. Since 1980, the US Department of Energy alone has spent over $12 billion on solar, geothermal, wind and other renewables, Rockefeller University environmental professor Jesse Ausubel points out. And these supplemental sources still provide just 4% of our energy mix.

Biomass may have the most negative environmental consequences. Using modern methods, farmers might be able to grow 4,800 thermal watts of biomass per acre, energy analyst Howard Hayden calculates. All that plant matter could then be burned to generate electricity.

By comparison, a typical 1,000-MW nuclear power plant (on about 100 acres) produces about 8 billion kilowatt hours of electricity in a year. To get that same amount of power from biomass, farmers would have to plant nearly 625,000 acres – 975 square miles, just slightly more than Rhode Island. To produce enough biomass to generate all the electricity the United States uses in a year, professor Ausubel estimates, we would have to plant an area *ten times the size of Iowa!*

This is land that could no longer be used to provide food for hungry people, forage for dairy cows or habitat for wildlife. Growing the biomass fiber would require enormous amounts of water ... as well as fertilizer, pesticides and tractor fuel that come from petroleum – which we must import or obtain from lands that legislators and courts continue to make off limits. And burning it would generate millions of tons of ash, soot, hydrocarbons and greenhouse gases.

It is considerations like these that have begun to turn ethanol "from panacea to pariah in the span of one growing season," says the *Wall Street Journal*. Even as Congress and the President talked of increasing US corn-based ethanol output to *15 billion gallons a year* by 2022, many people began to question the fuel's environmental bona fides and its ability to reduce foreign oil imports.

Our handling of this fuel is an object lesson in why we must never let hype and emotion take over, where careful economic and environmental analysis should control – and should *precede* any policy judgments and legislative enactments.

America planted 93 million acres in corn during 2006. That's equal to Illinois, Indiana and Iowa put together. One-sixth of this corn got turned into ethanol. And it took a huge amount of water, fertilizer, pesticides and diesel fuel to grow this corn, more diesel to transport it, and a lot of coal and natural gas to convert it into ethanol.

According to Environmental Defense (which supports fossil fuel resource lock-ups and promotes global warming chaos themes), it takes up to six gallons of water to produce a single gallon of ethanol. That translates into 90 billion gallons of water a year, from 2022 onward, if those new mandates go into effect. The impact on groundwater and surface water supplies alike would send repercussions through cities, habitats and food crops.

Diesel-burning trucks must haul the fuel to gas stations, since it can't be pipelined the way gasoline is – because ethanol picks up water, which can ruin your engine or cause it to stall. (That can be a serious problem, if you're in an airplane a few thousand feet up.) Ethanol blends can also rot out the fiberglass tanks in boats. Motorists pay more per tank for the fuel – but get 10% less mileage than from pure gasoline.

The Brookings Institute's Michael O'Hanlon says corn ethanol yields just 30% more energy than is required to produce the fuel. Analyst Michael Economides calculates that it took nearly 9 billion gallons of gasoline equivalent to get 5 billion gallons of ethanol in 2006. And Nobel-Prize-winning chemist Paul Crutzen co-authored a report that said corn-ethanol might actually worsen climate change, because fertilizers would increase emissions of nitrous oxide, a greenhouse gas.

Producing just the 7 billion gallons of ethanol we got in 2007 required some 22 million acres of prime farmland – an area nearly the size of Indiana. By comparison, the Arctic National Wildlife Refuge (ANWR) could produce some *21 billion gallons* of gasoline annually for 20 years from *just 2,000 acres* – one-twentieth of Washington, DC.

Congress happily acquiesced to all the environmental and other costs of converting corn into ethanol. But it has repeatedly refused to permit any drilling in ANWR, off our coasts, or in the Rocky Mountain West – for the oil and gas that belongs to *you and me,* not just to environmental elitists. This makes no sense.

Corn-based ethanol enriches certain farmers – but raises costs for cattle, pork, turkey and chicken farmers, as well as prices of meat, milk, soft drinks and countless other products. Poor families again get hit hardest.

In fact, corn prices soared from $2 a bushel for three decades – to an average of $3.35 per bushel in 2007, according to the Agriculture Department. Predictably, other farmers began to complain, as did packaged food companies, consumers and other organizations.

The Organization for Economic Cooperation and Development concluded that biofuels in general "offer a cure [for oil dependence] that is worse than the disease." The National Academy of Sciences underscored the threat to water supplies.

The liberal and activist American Lung Association worried about air pollutants from burning ethanol in gasoline. Mexico blamed US ethanol demand for soaring prices of corn tortillas, and the great humanitarian Fidel Castro said using food crops to produce fuel is "a sinister idea."

Even refining ethanol from sugar cane or switch grass (cellulosic ethanol) is now coming under fire from many experts. It's certainly preferable to corn-based ethanol, but farmers still have to grow, harvest, transport and process the biomass. That means taking millions of acres out of food crops and wildlife habitat to grow the plants … using billions of gallons of water and millions of tons of fertilizer and pesticides … and putting further upward pressure on food prices.

Wind power problems center around their intermittent, unreliable output, thumping and constant low-frequency noise, and massive land requirements. The American Wind Energy Association has claimed the United States could generate 20% of its electricity by dedicating "less than 1%" of its landmass to wind farms. That may sound attractive to people who see wind energy as an alternative to the 20% of our electricity that now comes from nuclear power plants.

However, 1% of the US is 23,000,000 acres – the entire state of Virginia. Meeting New York City's electricity needs alone would require a wind farm across the entire state of Connecticut, according to Ausubel. Meeting the United States' 2005 electricity demand with wind power would require blanketing *Texas and Louisiana* with turbines – that somehow would have to operate 24/7/365.

Few would say that covering this much land with noisy, 300-foot-tall wind turbines is an Earth-friendly alternative to nuclear power or fossil fuels. The turbines also kill raptors and other birds. Moreover, to be relatively effective, these towering "cuisinarts of the sky" (a Sierra Club term) would have to sit atop ridges, hills and escarpments, becoming a glaring visual blight across vast scenic vistas.

There are also dangers of potentially catastrophic mishaps. A recent report from Germany (where 19,000 wind turbines dot the landscape) recounted "thousands of mishaps, breakdowns and accidents," including fires, fractures in rotors and deterioration in concrete foundations. In several cases, 100-foot rotor blades broke or sheared off, sending pieces flying; in another, an entire structure simply folded in half. Denmark had to remove the turbines from an entire offshore wind park in 2004, because the turbines could not withstand sea and weather conditions.

Caution, regulation and inspection are clearly in order.

Because their output is intermittent, wind turbines require expensive coal- or gas-fired power plants that stand idle much of the time, but are ready to provide instantaneous substitute or supplemental electricity to ensure the continued operation of businesses, schools, factories, homes and essential services.

(The nuclear power plants that provide 20% of America's electricity together utilize roughly 73,000 acres. A 550-MW gas-fired plant occupies around 30 acres; such a power plant generates more electricity over the course of a year than all 13,000 of California's first-generation wind turbines, which occupy 106,000 acres, according to energy analysts.

Even a 1,600-MW mine-mouth coal-fired plant like the Prairie State Energy facility planned for southern Illinois would require only 3,000 acres – and that includes the adjacent coal mine that will provide its fuel.

It will use advance pulverized coal technology and state-of-the-art pollution controls, to generate abundant, reliable, affordable electricity for homes and businesses in the region.)

In short, wind energy *is* a good supplement to other sources of electricity. It is not an alternative to them.

Photovoltaic power also has a huge ecological footprint. A single 1,000-MWe plant would require 58 square miles (37,000 acres) – the land area of Washington, DC – says Ausubel. That's a lot of desert habitat to cover with black panels. (Let's make sure someone does a careful endangered species study ahead of time.) The system would also need expensive coal or gas backup generators, or a vast array of expensive batteries.

Last, there are the material needs. Some of the more efficient photovoltaic systems contain toxic elements like cadmium. Batteries to store electricity contain all kinds of metals. And the sheer volume of material needed to manufacture and erect a wind farm is daunting. According to Berkeley engineer Per Peterson, building and installing a wind farm takes five to ten times the steel and concrete that is required for a nuclear plant that generates the same amount of electricity – and does so more reliably.

Tradeoffs. Keep them in mind. There's no free lunch.

Continued progress and opportunity

Nevertheless, despite these costs, environmental impacts and other drawbacks, we still need renewable energy resources. We will need more of them in the coming decades. And they will be built – along with more coal, gas and nuclear power plants.

America runs on abundant, reliable, affordable energy. It is the "Master Resource" that creates economic opportunities and turns our constitutionally guaranteed civil rights into rights that we enjoy in reality. Never forget that.

Our energy system will grow and evolve – and we don't need massive subsidies or legislative mandates to make it happen. We certainly don't need congressional edicts and market-twisting laws that create all kinds of unintended and unwanted economic and ecological impacts.

What we really need is laws that let our free enterprise system work, encourage our risk takers and innovators, and unleash what economist Julian Simon called "our Ultimate Resource" – the brilliant, industrious, creative minds with which we have been blessed by our Creator.

That's what made America grow and prosper, and create wondrous opportunities in the past. It can do so again, if we let it.

The progress may come fitfully, incrementally and slowly. Or it may come through seemingly sudden breakthroughs, as with microwaves, cell phones and nuclear power.

Just take yourself back in time a mere century, to 1900 New York City – my home for 60 years. Coal and wood provided the heat. There was no AC. People froze in the winter, sweltered all summer, and died every day from tuberculosis and waterborne diseases. Over 120,000 horses provided the transportation – and left mountains of manure and thousands of carcasses to be hauled away every year. No wonder cars were hailed as pollution reducers, when they arrived a few years later.

Communication was by newspaper, telegraph or personal visit. Entertainment was a family affair or a trip to the local church or pub. Telephones, cars and electricity were novelties for the rich. The Wright brothers were still making bicycles. There was no television!

Not one person alive, not even Jules Verne, could have imagined the changes that were to come over the next century – radio, television and ipods, computers, air conditioning, gas and nuclear power, plastics, antibiotics, organ transplants, and on and on.

Not one person alive today can possibly envision the changes that will come during the next ten, fifty or one hundred years – at a much faster pace than ever before … in energy and transportation, pollution control, communication, medicine, and more.

We might invent radically new photovoltaic systems, solve the carbon dioxide dilemma, discover that solar and cosmic ray cycles really are the key to climate change. Newer, better nuclear reactor designs might soon power tar sand, oil shale and coal liquefaction processes that make the United States more self-sufficient in petroleum – while they also power hydrogen production processes that finally make de-carbonization and a hydrogen-based economy possible.

Want further proof?

Over the past 35 years, the US population grew by 40 percent. Our Gross Domestic Product by nearly 200 percent. Our miles traveled by 175 percent. Our electricity consumption by well over 100 percent. Coal burning went up 80 percent.

And yet, during this same period, our aggregate air pollution was *cut in half*, as a result of steady advances in energy efficiency and pollution control, air quality expert Joel Schwartz points out. Lead and certain other pollutants were reduced by 90 percent or more.

During 2006 alone, according to the Energy Information Administration, US greenhouse gas emissions fell 1.5 percent. Since 1990, our nation's GHG-intensity – our greenhouse emissions per unit of Gross Domestic Product – has declined an average of 2 percent a year, as our economy has grown and despite (or maybe because of) our refusal to sign the economy-killing Kyoto Protocol.

To me, that's great news, even though I don't believe in climate chaos disaster theories. And the progress continues, step by step.

Optimism, hard work, and faith in America, progress and our Ultimate Resource.

That's the job of the Energy Keepers.

PART 2

ENERGY KILLERS

CHAPTER 5
ENERGY GRAVEYARDS

"Starve America First" could be the environmentalist motto. We've got more energy imprisoned in "wilderness areas" and buried in "nature preserve" graveyards on our own soil than most nations have all together.

And environmental groups lobbied *every one of those areas* out of reach – with money from wealthy foundations, many of which hold substantial energy company stocks in their endowment portfolios. Think a moment about what could be out there:

> Federal lands hold an estimated 635 trillion cubic feet of recoverable natural gas, enough to heat the 60 million US homes that are powered by natural gas for 160 years.
> Federal lands also hold an estimated 112 billion barrels of recoverable oil, enough to produce gasoline for 60 million cars *and* fuel oil for 25 million homes for 60 years.

Those federal lands and resources are often referred to as "public" lands and resources, because they're owned by *all* Americans, for the benefit of *all* Americans. They're not owned only by well-off environmentalists, rich foundations and other elites – but by all of us.

And not just for the recreational or spiritual benefit of those elites – but for energy and jobs and tax revenues and vehicular recreation by Average Joes and Janes, as well. Somehow, though, the elites have taken control, and your rights and mine are being ignored and trampled on.

We often say the energy supply debate is about oil, and it is. But clean-burning natural gas is also essential to our economy. Just look again at the Energy Reality chart on page 3. US consumers use over 22 trillion cubic feet of natural gas every year, to generate electricity, keep warm and cool, travel, and make indispensable items like medicines, fertilizers and fabrics.

Natural gas is the cleanest fossil fuel and offers excellent home energy value. Using more of it will reduce greenhouse gas emissions, while giving us a bona fide, existing source of abundant, affordable, reliable energy. It's also vital if we want to rely more on intermittent, unreliable energy sources like wind and solar power.

Without gas-fired (or coal-fired) electricity generators that can kick in every time the wind stops blowing or sun stops shining, homes, offices, hospitals and equipment that are connected to the grid come to a grinding halt.

In some areas, wind-generated power interruptions can occur 50 to 200 times a year. Most of us have a fit when brownouts or blackouts occur a half dozen times a year. Fossil-fuel backup systems are absolutely essential with renewables.

By locking up our natural gas, radical environmentalists don't just raise your energy prices and interfere with your life and civil rights. They also strangle our emerging market for renewable (supplemental) energy. That's as basic as energy policy gets. But it's apparently too complex for most greens, judges and legislators to figure out.

Or else they're deliberately using these resource lockups to *force* us to "transform" our lifestyles and living standards, and surrender our energy and economic civil rights.

Global warming true believers should be shouting for more natural gas production. But they're not, because it's a fossil fuel. They'll do everything they can to destroy access to the natural gas beneath federal lands and coastal waters – and work against their own global warming ideology without noticing or acknowledging the schizophrenia.

Rationality has nothing to do with these people or this issue. It's just a swarm of beliefs, values, attitudes and dismissive waves of the hand – like "don't bother me with facts or the cries for justice of the disadvantaged."

In fact, sometimes I think environmentalists would rather see you jobless, homeless or even dead, than to support fossil fuel use, even the best, cleanest and most abundant.

To top it off, we're close to being energy independent in natural gas. Currently, 18 trillion cubic feet a year (or about 85%) of our natural gas comes from US sources. But it could, and should, be a lot more. Instead, our domestic production is slowly but steadily declining, as we use more and more every year (thanks in part to state and federal mandates and pollution control rules) and produce less and less (thanks mostly to land and resource lockups).

No, the debate's not just about oil. Securing our energy civil rights and gaining access to our domestic oil and natural gas will be a critical job for Energy Keepers in the coming years, and natural gas is going to be as contentious as oil, timber and mining.

The Rocky Mountain West alone contains an estimated 167 trillion cubic feet of recoverable natural gas. That's enough to heat 64 million homes for 40 years. But more than 40% of that – 69 trillion cubic feet of *your* natural gas – has been put off limits by environmentalist lobbying and legal actions. That means higher natural gas prices, more foreign imports and fewer jobs, thanks to the Sierra Club set.

In offshore America – the Outer Continental Shelf, or OCS – more than 85% of both oil and gas have been put off limits to exploration. By who else? Environmentalists in suits – and lawsuits. Only 24% of federal oil and gas prospects are actually available under standard lease terms, and many more areas are burdened with severe lease restrictions.

In the West Coast OCS, 21 trillion cubic feet of *your* natural gas have been put off limits by environmental lobbying and lawsuits.

In the East Coast's Outer Continental Shelf, 33 trillion cubic feet of *your* natural gas have been put under lock and key by environmentalist actions.

Off the Florida coast in the Gulf of Mexico, another 25 trillion cubic feet of *your* OCS natural gas are still being contested by environmentalists.

How much is that? At 2006 consumption levels, the 148 trillion cubic feet of natural gas that's already interred in our Nationwide Energy Graveyard could:

- Supply all industrial users for 23 years.
- Provide all the nation's gas-generated electricity for 24 years.
- Heat every gas-equipped residence in America for 34 years.
- Furnish commercial users for 53 years.
- Drive every one of America's natural-gas-fueled vehicles for 6,166 years!

But it won't. It won't heat or light or transport anybody or anything. Thanks to heedless, uncaring, well-off, well-fed environmentalists, it's in an energy graveyard that's beyond your reach or mine. That's not right.

Here's another sample. In Colorado's Roan Plateau, 15 trillion cubic feet of your natural gas (if you believe Bureau of Land Management geologists) or half a trillion (if you believe Wilderness Society lobbyists) have been targeted for a development "moratorium" of 15 to 20 years because of environmentalist pressure tactics.

What about oil? In Alaska's Arctic National Wildlife Refuge (ANWR), at least 4.5 billion barrels of *your* oil (and possibly as much as 11.5 billion barrels) have been kept off limits by environmentalist lies, lobbying and litigation.

This oil could be brought out of the ground and sent to refineries and your gas tank via the Trans-Alaska Pipeline (TAP). Drilling would be done in wintertime, across ice roads that melt in the spring. Wildlife would barely notice the activities. Total land actually affected by the drilling pads, local pipelines and other facilities would be about 2,000 acres – one-twentieth of the land area of Washington, DC.

Developing ANWR oil would also extend life of the huge Prudhoe Bay oil field by several years and several billion barrels of *your* oil – because it would ensure that there's enough oil to keep TAP flowing. Without ANWR, in a few years, even sophisticated and expensive advanced oil recovery techniques won't produce enough oil to keep the pipeline operating , and we'd have to leave huge amounts of *your* recoverable oil in the ground. That's the opposite of energy conservation – something environmentalists are supposedly in favor of.

That's just part of the problem with environmentalists. The whole list would fill a book. In fact, the US government has filled *many* books with surveys, budgets, studies, lawsuit transcripts and congressional testimony about America's buried energy treasures. In fact, federal land management agencies report that about 40% of their annual budget goes to pay for lawsuits filed by environmentalists to stop development of *your* lands, *your* resources and *your* energy.

That's not just disgusting. It's infuriating. It's anti-poor, and it violates basic energy and economic civil rights.

Instead of helping you get abundant, reliable, affordable energy – under rules and procedures that protect wildlife and the environment – well-off environmentalist lawyers, tacticians and lobbyists repeatedly shed their Birkenstocks and T-shirts for dress-up days in court or congressional hearings, to keep *your* energy away from you and your children.

There's a certain mentality that goes with this noxious game of keep-away. You could call it the Wilderness Mind. In fact, the Wilderness Act of 1964 itself was the brainchild of such a mind – that of an environmentalist named Howard Zahnizer, who was head of the Wilderness Society from 1945 until his death in 1964. He lobbied Congress for 15 years to create the National Wilderness Preservation System, a bureaucratic grab bag into which an endless amount of federal land could be inserted.

Zahnizer's 1964 Wilderness Act was a way to stop all development, energy included. By law, wilderness can't have roads, structures (not even toilets or primitive shelters), or mechanized vehicles (not even bicycles or wheelchairs). Wilderness law allows backpacking, hunting, fishing, horseback riding and scientific research. That's it. Certainly not energy development.

What's more, the National Wilderness Preservation System is also infinitely elastic.

In fact, Congress launched the National Wilderness Preservation System with just 9 million acres. It envisioned a top limit of about 15 million acres. As of 2007, there were 106 million acres in the system, with millions more waiting for congressional approval. Greedy empire builders should study America's Wilderness System.

106 million acres is more than the entire state of California. It's almost equal to Virginia, North and South Carolina and Georgia put together. And much of this land is loaded with oil, gas and all kinds of minerals – including many that we never needed before but may need if we want the high-tech "renewable" energy future that greens and politicians keep promising.

But even that isn't enough. The elastic law has been twisted and stretched to mean that even being able to *see* an oil rig (or even the lights from a rig at night) interferes with the "wilderness experience" of hypersensitive backpackers.

So the noisy, relentless pressure groups have managed to create no-drilling "buffer zones" around a lot of areas, to "protect" wildlife and ensure that pampered hikers don't have unexpected encounters with civilization.

Zahnizer's law obviously did a good job killing energy development. He was a true nature purist. That's someone who loves nature – and *only* nature – plus maybe a spouse and a few like-minded friends. But definitely not folks like you and me who *use* things. God forbid.

Groups like the Sierra Club and the National Wildlife Federation, like Environmental Defense and the Natural Resources Defense Council, brag about how much land they control now, and how much energy they've kept from the people who own it – people like you and me.

Well, you might say, that can't be too much, can it?

Yes, my friend, it can. The federal government owns nearly 650 million acres of land – almost one third of the land area of the United States, including Alaska and Hawaii. That means the feds own nearly one out of every three acres in this supposedly capitalist, private property-loving country.

There's a lot of coal and oil and gas beneath those one-in-three government acres. States, counties and families depend on it for their energy, recreation and livelihoods.

Federally-owned and managed lands include National Parks, National Monuments, National Forests, National Wildlife Refuges, National Wild and Scenic Rivers, National Trails and several dozen other National This and Thats.

The theory is that these lands are held for all Americans. The reality is that these lands are held for affluent, highly educated, white, politically-savvy environmentalists.

They're the ones who lobbied for the maze of federal regulations which ensure that you and I don't get a drop of energy out of *our* ground without some hard-working technician filling out hundreds of forms, waiting months and even years, enduring "public comment" campaigns financed by rich activists, fighting lawsuits by "local citizen groups" with money from a thousand miles away, and then when (or *if*) the permit gets approved, trying to keep his company's equipment safe from eco vandals while they get a little energy for us.

Environmentalists think they own the federal lands. I think it's time to teach them otherwise.

I saw a government website (www.nationalatlas.gov) that said: "The Federal agencies responsible for managing America's natural resources must meet both the public desire to protect them and the public expectation of economic growth based on them."

That got me to thinking. There's a huge mass movement to "protect" government lands, literally thousands of well-financed environmental groups – all of them intent on locking up energy and opposing the "public expectation   of economic growth" based on the resources on and under those publicly owned lands.

But where's the constituency for "the public expectation of economic growth" – for the resources needed to make growth and opportunity possible? When was the last time you saw a Discovery Channel program that featured a gravel-voice narrator extolling the value of energy, in a beautifully filmed love-song to oil drilling in Colorado, or gas development somewhere in Wyoming, or coal mining in Escalante, Utah – so that people can enjoy fulfilling lives that aren't nasty, brutish and short? Or featuring the absolutely spectacular marine habitats found beneath offshore oil and gas production platforms, off the coasts of Texas, Louisiana and California?

I think our constituency is out there, all over America. I think it just doesn't know it yet. Because a lot of people don't know how much of their energy is buried, or where.

They don't know the graveyard stories.

Let me tell you one. It might be the most outrageous story of all.

It recounts the saga of President Bill Clinton's proclamation that "en-graved" the world's biggest deposit of clean, low-sulfur coal – coal that could have fueled power plants across America's Midwest and Southwest for decades, with very little pollution.

Coal is a vital part of our Energy Reality mix. It provides half of all the electricity we use – *20% of all the energy that runs America*. That electricity is becoming more important every year: for lighting, heating and cooling … for computers and other consumer and industrial electronics … for lasers and other medical devices that improve and safeguard our health … as a primary energy source for numerous industrial applications. And if we are truly going to shift gradually to electric cars, we will need even more reliable electrical power.

Wind and solar just aren't ready for prime time yet, and won't be more than a minor supplemental energy source for decades – even if we're ready to blanket millions of acres with towering turbines and sacrifice thousands of raptors and other birds. Natural gas is essential for home heating and as a feedstock for fertilizers, plastics, pharmaceuticals and other products –

and we continue to build gas-fired generating plants. But it's more expensive than coal, and environmental pressure groups have put vast deposits off limits to the people who own them.

So coal is still king. America has 235 years' worth of coal, at current levels of use.

Even California understands these Energy Realities. It plans to slash greenhouse gas emissions from within its borders, but it doesn't plan to destroy its economy in the process. So it's backing plans for huge new coal-fired electrical generating plants. Those plants will be special in two ways.

They'll be state-of-the-art, low-polluting and thus very expensive. And they'll be built, not in California, but in Idaho, Montana, Utah and Wyoming. That way, the Golden State gets to have its electricity cake (via a 2,000-mile-long high tension power line to Los Angeles) and eat it too (by keeping its own greenhouse emissions within its highly promoted statutory limits). I call it the No-Pain, All-Perception Diet for the Climate.

The fact is, power plants fueled by coal are far less polluting than 30 years ago. Just since 1998, their annual sulfur dioxide emissions and nitrogen oxide have declined another 28% and 43% respectively – and new rules require large additional reductions that will eliminate most remaining emissions by 2015.

Coal-fired power plants are now the primary source of US mercury emissions only because the major sources (incinerating wastes and processing ores containing mercury) have been eliminated. US mercury emissions are now down 82% since the early 1980s; America accounts for only 2% of all global mercury emissions; 55% of global emissions come from volcanoes, oceans and forest fires; and two-thirds of mercury deposition in America comes from other countries. Nevertheless, new EPA rules require a further 70% reduction in mercury from power plants by 2015.

That leaves CO_2 and catastrophic climate change as a rationale for opposing coal. But the science behind climate chaos claims is questionable, and the social and economic costs of implementing draconian "global warming prevention" schemes would be horrendous.

The question is, will we be able to use it? Or will Energy Killers lock up our coal too, and price or regulate available deposits out of reach? Back to our story.

The year was 1996. The coal, 7 billion tons of it, worth about a trillion dollars, was in southwestern Utah. The proclamation – a presidential power conferred by the obscure Antiquities Act of 1906 and not used for nearly 20 years – created the 1.7-million-acre Grand Staircase-Escalante National Monument, setting aside a playground far larger than Delaware for the environmental elite.

National monuments aren't big statues or imposing architectural masterpieces, as the name seems to indicate. They're interesting natural areas that don't quite make the grade as national parks.

The first one was the impressive volcanic core in Wyoming called Devil's Tower. It starred in Steven Spielberg's 1977 science fiction movie, *Close Encounters of the Third Kind*.

It was proclaimed a national monument by President Theodore Roosevelt in 1906. It only covers a little more than 1,300 acres. That was the kind of thing the 1906 law was intended to protect.

In Clinton's monster 1.7-million-acre Grand Staircase-Escalante National Monument and Energy Graveyard, the Dutch firm Andalex Resources held a small 3,400-acre mining lease, which the government supposedly had to honor. But the feds told the company they didn't have to grant the road permits the company would need to get the coal out, and they weren't about to do so. Andalex gave up. Now the only similar coal deposit on Earth was already under development in South Kalimantan, Indonesia.

That raised suspicions. Clinton had substantial connections with Indonesia's $6-billion Lippo Group conglomerate, founded by financial magnate Mochtar Riady, an ethnic Chinese born in Indonesia. Clinton granted Riady and his son James numerous White House meetings; beginning in 1991, Lippo executives gave $700,000 to the Democratic Party. Most interesting, Lippo's Hong Kong bank had a memorandum of understanding with a 1,200-megawatt Chinese coal firm. Connecting the dots, reporter Sarah Foster of Sacramento proposed that Clinton buried Utah's coal to kill off a competitor to his Indonesian friends.

It makes an interesting conspiracy theory, but that wasn't what happened at all. That would have been mere greed. The truth is much worse: environmental ideologues manipulating the president of the United States into blindly damaging America's energy self-sufficiency under the pretext of polishing his green credentials in a problematic election year. But nobody knew that until Congress got a subpoena and sent federal marshals to the White House, to seize the secret memos and emails that revealed the *real* conspiracy.

The seized documents told a chilling story. It began in the summer of 1995, when an environmentalist named Ken Rait of the Southern Utah Wilderness Alliance (SUWA) escorted Kathleen ("Katie") McGinty for two weeks through the area that would become the national monument. McGinty was Clinton's chair of the President's Council on Environmental Quality, and a very savvy political operator.

SUWA wanted a 5-million-acre Wilderness declared in the area.

However, that would require an Act of Congress, and Congress was now in Republican hands.

McGinty sympathized with the wilderness idea, but it was too big and too controversial.

She and Rait both knew that the proclamation power of the Antiquities Act could trump Congress: a national monument didn't need congressional authorization the way a Wilderness area did. They both knew Bill Clinton was in trouble with the environmental movement for going along with a timber program they disliked. They both knew a presidential election year was coming soon.

When McGinty returned to Washington, she hatched a convoluted plot to convince the president that he needed to make a bold move to regain the environmental vote. In a series of tricks that Clinton knew nothing about, McGinty developed the national monument project in tight secrecy. She got the proclamation drafted without word getting out to anyone.

Utah's congressional delegation didn't know. Utah's Governor Michael Leavitt didn't know. Even White House Chief of Staff Leon Panetta didn't know.

When word was carefully leaked out that the president would soon announce a new national monument for Utah, Governor Leavitt frantically flew to Washington for a meeting with Clinton – who was out campaigning in Illinois.

Leon Panetta and Katie McGinty met with Leavitt, who told them to hold off, that his state planners had been working on what to do in the area for years, and it wasn't just the coal that would vanish into a national monument. It was also huge chunks of "state school lands" that federal law had designated in Utah (and other largely federal-owned Western states) to provide revenue for public schools. They would get put off limits, with no road access to them either, and billions of dollars in royalties and taxes would be lost, along with countless jobs.

After Panetta saw what was at stake, he told Leavitt, "Stay by the phone." When Leavitt left, Panetta told McGinty the president had to hold off, it was too important. She threw a snit, threatened to resign, shouted that it was the right thing to do and, besides, everything was arranged and it was too late to stop now.

Panetta caved in and let the president deal with it later that night.

It was 2 in the morning when Leavitt's motel phone rang. "Governor, the president of the United States." They talked for half an hour, but even after learning the magnitude of the problem – which came as a total surprise – Clinton wouldn't hold off his public announcement. He merely agreed to Leavitt's recommendation to "form a commission" to work out the details after the proclamation was issued and it was all a done deal.

Utah's congressional delegation was steamed. It made it clear the president was not welcome in their state to destroy a good part of their economy and their future. So the big event was held across the Arizona state line, on the South Rim of the Grand Canyon.

The location was kept under wraps. Utah government officials were clueless. But every environmentalist of note, including movie star Robert Redford, knew where to be.

Now let's think about all of that.

Nobody elected Kathleen McGinty. She was an appointee in a bureau few Americans ever heard of. She had come from the staff of Senator Al Gore.

Katie McGinty was networked with everybody of importance in the environmental movement. One of those people was head of a little-known Utah environmental group. While on a two-week vacation, she visited an area the environmental group was interested in locking up as wilderness.

A year later, she had manipulated the highest officer in the land to bury a trillion dollars worth of clean coal and innumerable economic opportunities – to fulfill her ideology.

She killed *your* energy.

Contrary to her righteous indignation, that's *not* the right thing to do. It was wrong. Flat, dead wrong.

Suppose McGinty had been in cahoots with a mining company, instead. Suppose she had worked out a deal to open a mine in the middle of Utah's Bryce Canyon National Park. All hell would have broken loose – and rightly so.

There's a right way and a wrong way to do things in this country – openly, honestly, transparently and with accountability. But apparently, if you're an environmentalist, even if you're a government official, those rules don't apply.

Don't you think it's time the same rules applied to everyone?

Don't you think it's time we got your coal out of that energy graveyard?

That's the job of the Energy Keepers.

CHAPTER 6
KILLING OIL AND GAS

If you've come this far, you know what our energy and political problems are, you know about the phony climate change problem and something of the energy graveyards and who dug them. Now you need to learn a lot more about the Energy Killers.

I wouldn't have believed such people could exist, if it hadn't been for a magazine article a friend sent me. And I've seen more than my share of environmental zealots, who are totally oblivious about the disadvantaged and don't care who they hurt – even the millions of African mothers and babies who died after the zealots banished DDT from malaria-control programs.

You can find mobs of such self-absorbed militants in all kinds of movements.

But this was something beyond zealots screaming in your face about how bad you are for using fossil fuels and hurting the Earth, as if you have no right to be here, and are "a cancer on the Earth," as some of them have put it.

This magazine article outlined a cold-blooded, hard-hearted, well-planned *elimination* of the fossil fuel industry in America. And with it the elimination of the living standards, jobs, opportunities and civil rights that those fossil fuels provide. And, yes, "elimination" is the right word.

The article was just a single page, torn out of a trade journal called the *American Oil and Gas Reporter*. The article was called "Group Sets Plan To Stop Oil And Gas." I expected the usual Corporate Social Responsibility public relations nonsense about the wonders of going green. That's not what this article was about.

It was about a group of radical environmental organizations that have already launched a program that they are absolutely certain is going to stop, eliminate, eradicate oil and gas drilling, development, production and pipeline operations in the Western United States.

Not just planning to stop, or hoping, or maybe. *Certainty* that they would succeed. Not just a particular well or project. *An entire industry* – and all the jobs that go with it, all the families it supports, directly and indirectly. A kind of ethnic or social cleansing – like what they've done to the timber industry out West and are trying to do to ranching.

The article began:

> A multiyear strategy "to reform the operations of the oil and gas industry in the United States" is revealed in a document distributed at the June 12 meeting of the Liaison Committee of Cooperating Oil & Gas Associations.

I didn't know who this "Liaison Committee" was, or even who is represented by this "Cooperating Oil & Gas Associations." But I do know what that clever, sanitized word "reform" means when used by ideologues to cloak their schemes in the language of "protecting the environment" and "safeguarding the public interest." That's what they said about DDT, too.

The true meaning is closer to "*de*form" than to "*re*form," and it's usually synonymous with "destroy" or "demolish" or "dismantle." To figure out their real meaning and intention, you just have to ask the same questions we asked earlier – the same ones you need to ask every time one of these outfits says it's a "stakeholder" and wants to "protect" us, by "preventing" some newly discovered "crisis."

1. Will their "publicly spirited" campaign give us more energy – or less?
2. Will it lower energy prices – or raise them?

The article went on to say this large coalition of nongovernmental organizations had already coalesced around a six-year strategy that includes an emphasis on climate change – but will increasingly focus on oil and gas operations all over our western states. The real highlight will be "an over-arching, multi-issue strategy focused on ... oil and gas operations." And the strategy was all laid out in a secret document.

Translated into plain English, this means a big, un-named coalition of non-profit, tax-exempt, radical environmental groups has committed their multi-million-dollar donors, their ferocious political clout, and their friends in Congress and state legislatures to "reforming" the operations of the oil and gas industry – first out West, and probably then all over the United States.

Now I was getting worried. How did the magazine know this? What did this "document" actually say? Where did it come from? Was it reliable? The magazine only said the document was obtained by the Colorado Oil & Gas Association, and it outlines an organized campaign that has been styled NoDOG, or "No Dirty Oil and Gas."

Several phone calls later, all I had learned was that this "NoDOG Memo," as it was known, had been circulating in the oil and gas and coal industries since late 2006.

Nobody knew who wrote it.

Nobody would say how they got it.

Nobody knew who all was in this "group" or who were the masterminds and financial brokers behind it.

It took me a week to find somebody who would even send me a copy of the actual NoDog Memo.

It was so incredible that I could hardly believe it. You won't either, which is why I've included it as Appendix B in this book.

Was it authentic?

It was obviously written by an environmental insider. There was too much detail for it to be a hoax. What cinched it in my mind, was this: by the time I got it, four or five of its early-2007 "reforms" had already been passed, exactly as predicted in the 2006 NoDOG Memo.

Whoever this "large coalition of nongovernmental organizations" was, they clearly had the power and money to do what the memo said.

That was serious, because several more years of devastating NoDOG projects had already been laid out. If carried out successfully, the NoDOG strategy would indeed stop oil and gas – and probably coal – in America.

I cannot express how arrogant and destructive this plan is. These self-righteous radicals would ruin businesses, families, savings and access to energy all over America. Every decent American should rise up in anger against them. It affects the energy and economic civil rights of every one of us.

The memo's author must have felt at least a twinge of worry, anger, doubt and guilt, or he/she would never have written it. The insider clearly believed in the coalition's general and more rational goals to protect the environment – but just as clearly felt very nervous about the coalition's determination to ignite a real and deadly energy Armageddon.

The writer talked about "the environmentalists" who will do this or that. He or she didn't say "we" will do this or that. The writer talked about "they plan" – not "we plan." There was a clear distancing in the language.

It was the work of a true believer whose beliefs had been exceeded and then betrayed by fanatical colleagues, and foundation directors who plan and finance so many eco attacks today.

The NoDOG Memo was the work of a decent human being, who had strong beliefs but still had enough of a conscience to recognize the horrible consequences of a plan that had spiraled out of control. It was the product of a guilty conscience – an attempt to gain redemption.

It took me a month of calling every friend I had who might know anything about the energy industry, but I finally located the person who had received the NoDOG Memo.

Our source would not allow his name to be used for obvious reasons. We'll just call him Deep Ear (I know it's lame, but cut me some slack here). I checked Deep Ear's credentials and verified reliability. Deep Ear has many years of experience in the energy field, including some government positions. Deep Ear's resume makes you want to meet the person it's about, just to see what Superman looks like.

Deep Ear has had long contact with just about every anti-energy activist in the West, if not in the whole country, as well as practically everybody in the energy industry.

Deep Ear has built a strong reputation for integrity at both ends of this political spectrum, and would have been an obvious choice to receive the NoDOG Memo – but only to someone high enough in the environmental movement's leadership to have been at many of the same energy conferences.

Deep Ear will confirm that assessment, but will not discuss it.

Deep Ear adamantly refuses to do anything that would endanger the source of the NoDOG Memo.

Did you get the memo in person, by postal mail, by email? No comment.

Did you get it from a man or a woman? No comment.

Is it a Rocky Mountain Westerner or someone from New York, Washington, or San Francisco? No comment.

Does Deep Ear know which groups are in the "large coalition?" No, Deep Ear does not.

Will Deep Ear ask the memo's author? No, Deep Ear will not.

Figuring out who the NoDOG players are and who's behind them looked like a guessing game.

Except for a loose thread hanging in the memo itself. It does mention one group – and only one: the Oil and Gas Accountability Project.

It was time to call a researcher I knew from working together in 2005 on a CORE project that advocates including DDT and other insecticides to help control malaria and save lives in Uganda. That little project is funded in part by ExxonMobil, which also operates its own $85 million malaria control program in Nigeria and other parts of Africa.

The researcher's name is Ron Arnold, and he's the executive vice president of the Center for the Defense of Free Enterprise. He's also the nation's top sleuth in tracking down non-profit groups and the money behind them. He filled me in on more details, and confirmed that my concerns were valid.

"Save yourself some fuss," Ron advised. "Don't think of NoDOG as a group, or even a 'large coalition' of groups.

"It's *a strategy*, a plan, a set of tactics.

"Sure, the strategy has a lot of followers, big groups, little groups, driven by money from big foundations and little foundations. I'll send you a list of the most obvious ones.

"Just keep in mind, Roy, it's a *strategy.* Any group can follow it. Don't think of it as No Dirty Oil and Gas, NoDOG. It's against coal, too. It's against fossil fuels, period.

"Think of it as No-ENERGY."

Our energy and economic civil rights are in far more danger than we had realized.

Countering the Energy Killers is the job of the Energy Keepers.

CHAPTER 7
NO-ENERGY TACTICS

So, NoDOG is a *strategy*, not a group or even a large coalition of groups. It's the No-Energy Strategy.

The NoDOG Memo draws a picture of the strategy that looks something like this:

Opening words: "A large coalition of NGOs has coalesced around a six-year strategy to reform the operations of the oil and gas industry in the United States. This strategy includes the current emphasis on climate change but increasingly will focus on oil and gas operations in the US West."

I presume that "reform" is the usual euphemism for "sabotage" or "destroy."

The plan begins in 2006 with deceptive messages aimed at small independent oil and gas providers in the Rocky Mountain West that don't suspect they are being targeted and don't have the financial resources for sustained battles.

Memo: "The first phase will look like a traditional public interest information / awareness campaign, but its end goal will be to establish a baseline set of standards for oil and gas operations."

Those "baseline standards" will actually be expensive "best practices" rules to cripple companies with costly new methods under the banner of "do it right" – even though the new rules will do little or nothing to improve environmental quality or protect public lands and resources.

Simultaneously, several dozen groups in the coalition begin to lobby for state and federal laws that *forbid* drilling, ostensibly to "protect" federal acreage, prevent global warming, save wildlife or "preserve the outdoor experience" – but actually to put more land into energy graveyards.

The "baseline standards" campaign will escalate.

Memo: "companies will be asked to meet the standard or improve upon it or face a market campaign (public attacks on the company from the entire broad coalition of NGOs)."

Presumably, the list of the "entire broad coalition" was scary enough to make company owners worry about how much bad publicity they could survive.

2007: A leading group in the coalition will launch a new anti-corporate campaign website. They have www.nodirtyoilandgas.org reserved for this purpose.

One of the coalition's groups will "issue a report outlining problems with current oil and gas operations."

Memo: The coalition "will recruit 'victim groups' who can be profiled in the report and who can be called upon to testify at the state and federal level." You can bet neither your "victim group" nor mine will be recruited. The whole thing is rigged – a setup.

Memo: Leaders "will broaden the coalition to increase the number of traditional Republican constituencies and hook-and-bullet [hunting and fishing] enthusiasts," to hide the partisan intent of the strategy. If they can't find any, they'll invent some.

Not surprisingly, When these "Republican" constituencies did show up, they were massively Democrat, including the so-called "Union Sportsmen's Alliance" of 20 labor unions that said they liked to hunt and fish, but seemed to spend more time jamming the halls of Congress for anti-energy committee hearings.

Memo: "In a media campaign, the coalition will publicize the relationship between the negative effects of oil and gas operations and specific products, including gasoline and plastics." Yeah, and other "evil" things we don't need, like jobs and heat and food.

The coalition lobbies anti-energy laws onto the books in New Mexico, Colorado, and Montana, and pressures Wyoming to tighten its existing laws. These new state laws were in fact passed in early 2007 and became the platform for forcing companies to operate under costly new restrictions, even in states that have no such laws.

The coalition lobbies new wilderness areas in New Mexico (Valle Vidal), obtains a rule to forbid drilling in a scenic area in Colorado (Roan Plateau), and presses for no-drilling "habitat protection" measures for endangered species" throughout the Rocky Mountain West.

All coalition messages emphasize the damage allegedly done by oil and gas development to wildlife, scenery, traffic, noise, neighbors, health and communities – while pretending to be improving the industry. They never mention the *benefits*, including energy, jobs, tax revenues, and grants to health, culture, education and the arts.

When mentioning benefits becomes unavoidable, as in congressional hearings, No-Energy activists dismiss them as "well, that's just old moneybags protecting his ill-gotten gains." And your job, car and mortgage payment, living standards, transportation, et cetera.

The coalition solicits nature magazines to publish drilling site photos aimed at upsetting nature lovers. This becomes a sustained publicity campaign to make the public fear and hate the oil and gas industry.

It's disingenuous, but it works.

Most drill sites are small – a few acres out of a thousand – and most never find oil or gas. They are quickly reclaimed, and a few years later you're hard pressed to find them. Actual production sites are mostly inconspicuous: a small wellhead or pipeline valve sticking out of the grass and brush. With modern directional drilling and production methods, even the big finds don't affect much acreage. If a bad actor doesn't clean up, it gets fined, and someone re-vegetates the area. But the stories and carefully framed photos never mention these facts.

By contrast, when we have a *real* disaster – like Mt. Saint Helens or the Yellowstone fires, which devastated hundreds of thousands of acres – the activists and magazines go into overdrive, to emphasize how miraculously Mother Nature rejuvenates the stricken areas. It will actually take decades to return them to forestland, but the articles rejoice over the wondrous natural recovery, and close-up photos turn every solitary flower or seedling into a miracle.

The broad coalition amasses a war-chest of millions in elitist foundation grants to begin the final phase of the No-Energy Strategy.

The "baseline standards" develop into a No-Energy "code of conduct" that sounds lofty and inspirational, but contains so many hidden expenses that good-faith compliance would eventually bankrupt any business that actually tried to obey the No-Energy code.

Memo: "By 2009, the coalition hopes to have led at least one company to have signed on to the code of conduct. It will then present the code of conduct and a selection of new state laws to Congress as the basis for the argument that the federal government is far behind industry and the states in protecting the public from oil and gas operations. The market campaign and the state laws, then, will together form the basis for a new federal law governing oil and gas."

The Memo ends on that "high point."

That is as cold-blooded an attack on a vital segment of society as I have ever seen, and I've seen a few.
What are we to make of this? Let's take it a little at a time.

You probably noticed that the NoDOG Memo emphasized *federal lands,* with state lands an important but distant second. That makes sense for several reasons. For one, federal rules are already so complicated that lobbying for more regulations on federal lands seems like business as usual, and not a deliberate effort to destroy our domestic energy industry. So it's a useful, effective and pernicious mask.

But it makes sense for other, not-so-obvious reasons. Most of America's domestic oil and gas drilling companies are small independents, not big corporate giants, and *about half of their operations are on federal lands*. That makes them especially vulnerable to activist attack: they have to comply with nightmarish federal rules already, and don't have the vast financial resources of a Shell or BP to endure more bureaucratic delays, fight continual environmentalist lawsuits against every new drilling permit, or bear the expense of endless, costly new "best practices" rules.

Independents are Little Oil, not Big Oil. They don't own refineries or filling stations, they have an average of only 12 employees, their average time in business is 23 years, and many are family operations. The American dream.

But here's why they're the most important target for Energy Killers: independents drill *90 percent of our new oil and gas wells*, produce *82 percent of our natural gas* and *68 percent of US oil*. Only half of their operations are on federal lands, but if you can bankrupt them there, they won't be available to drill for oil and gas anywhere else. Then the Energy Killers won't just have turned one-third of America's land into a vast energy graveyard. They will have effectively dismantled the bulk of the crews that drill elsewhere. They will have killed production of your vitally needed oil and gas all over the country.

Shut down these independent oil companies, and thousands of workers will lose their jobs. There are 125,000 Little Oil employees in the Rocky Mountain States alone. These good, hard-working people are being marginalized, demonized and destroyed by self-centered eco-bigots who look down on them as less deserving, less than human in fact – as a despised minority, and I know what that's like.

For every one of those 125,000 oil field workers who loses his or her job, *four other people*, **half a million other people altogether**, will lose theirs: grocery checkout clerks, teachers, nurses and others – because *every one of the primary workers supports four such workers.*

And when the Energy Killers shut down these jobs, they also shut down millions of dollars in tax and royalty revenues to communities, states and the federal government. They wipe out the energy that millions of people saved through hard conservation efforts, because every barrel they saved will be offset by a barrel that the Energy Killers have buried in energy graveyards Out West. They wipe out the energy that you and I and all Americans need.

The Energy Killers claim that we'll replace these *real* energy sources with the Sustainable New Energy Economy. There is no such thing. Read the Energy Reality chart again. Read Chapter 4 again. It's wishful thinking now, and for a long time to come. Maybe some day in the distant future, these imaginary energy sources may finally become reality. Until then, though, all these real people, real jobs and real revenues will just be more road kill.

And who will hold these Energy Killers accountable? These radical activists, their foundation puppet masters and bankers, the bureaucrats, judges and legislators who do their bidding – who will hold them accountable? What justice will we get for the heartless bigotry that destroys these jobs, revenues, opportunities, neighborhoods and civil rights?

That's the No-Energy Strategy:
America the Powerless. Fiendish.

That hits me hard. But you know what hit me hardest in reading the NoDOG Memo? It's *how much these Energy Killer activists know about the technical and legal details of oil and gas providers.* They have obviously spent years doing nothing but learning all about America's energy industry, not to help it supply the nation's vital needs, *but to destroy it.* And destroy the companies, industries and families that depend on abundant, reliable, affordable energy.

These Bull Connor Energy Killers obviously had some expert teachers and lawyers – not to mention some deep-pocket donors to pay their way while they wrecked other peoples' jobs, opportunities and dreams, and our national security.

We Energy Keepers don't have that advantage. We're not trust fund babies. We're people who have to work for a living. We use energy, and we don't take our jobs or our energy for granted. We can't spend years learning how to put the Energy Killers out of business, and we're not going to find experts to teach us how. For one thing, I don't think anybody knows how to challenge these nasty, wealthy 500-pound gorillas, and come away in one piece.

We have to rely on our sense of right and wrong, our sense of morality and responsibility, to counter them. We have to use their own tactics against them, and *make them live up to a code of conduct*, an Energy Keepers Code of Conduct.

We have to reframe the debate. It's not about the environment. We all care about and protect our environment. So do the Energy Providers. The real debate is over civil rights – yours and mine ... and civil wrongs – the ones committed by Energy Killers.

The second thing that struck me about the NoDOG memo? The only group in the "large coalition of NGOs" that's actually named in the memo, the "Oil and Gas Accountability Project" (OGAP for short), turns out to be a little group with big clout.

That seems highly unlikely – impossible even – unless you know that the entire environmental movement is highly incestuous. The same dozen groups are run by the same dozen activists and foundations. It's a few people, a lot of political connections, and a lot of money.

7 ♣
LEAN
Louisiana
Environmental
Action Network

6 ♣
Citizens
Coal
Council

5 ♣
VER BASIN
urce Council

8 ♣
WYOM
OUTD
COU

9 ♣
OIL AND GAS
ACCOUNTABILITY
PROJECT

6 ♣
BASIN
WATCH

2 ♣
VERMONT
LAW SCHO

3 ♣
Sustainable
Obtainable
Solutions

One Group's Directors Are Other Groups' Activists

OGAP's clout comes from its incestuous relations with other environmental groups: six of its seven directors also serve in some other anti-energy organization – which multiplies OGAP's clout by six (opposite). The only director who doesn't work elsewhere, its executive director, came from a little group called the San Juan Citizens Alliance (and before that from the activist Western Colorado Congress), and she carried that clout with her to OGAP.

Its board is comprised of leaders from the Wyoming Outdoor Council, Louisiana Environmental Action Network, Citizens Coal Council, Powder River Basin Resource Council, Great Basin Mine Watch, Sustainable Obtainable Solutions, and the Environmental Law Center at Vermont Law School. No, I never heard of them either.

The rest of OGAP's clout comes from foundation donors. OGAP was founded in 1999, got its IRS tax exemption in 2001, and is based in Durango, Colorado, a modest mountain town of about 14,000 population. Of its eleven foundation donors:

4 are in New York;
2 are in Connecticut (one of them gave OGAP $650,000);
2 are in Washington State;
1 is in Oregon;
1 is in New Mexico;
1 is in Colorado (in wealthy Aspen, and it gave less than $20,000).

But OGAP's real foundation clout didn't come from one of its own donors at all. It was a grant to a much larger group, a Washington, DC outfit called the Mineral Policy Center, which is an anti-mining group founded in 1988. In 2004, a Seattle-based foundation gave the Mineral Policy Center a large grant to change its name to Earthworks and merge with OGAP. Earthworks agreed to expand its program from anti-mining campaigns, to include anti-oil-and-gas campaigns, using OGAP's cunning, experience and instinct for the jugular.

Now they're the same setup, really. Earthworks has received grants from 36 foundations, mostly in the East, and OGAP now gets the benefit.

It would be bad enough if that's all there was to the No-Energy Strategy, but it's barely the beginning. When Ron Arnold sent me his list of "the most obvious players," I was appalled, because it kept showing me bigger and bigger organizations with more and more finances to throw at America's domestic energy providers. And Ron emphasized that it wasn't the whole "large coalition of NGOs," because they don't advertise their No-Energy Strategy membership. And they do a good job of preventing anyone from finding out.

But we do know that one of the first things that the Oil and Gas Accountability Project did after the merger was to hold a workshop in Denver titled *Corporate Energy Campaigning: Using Financial Pressure for Conservation.* It may have been where the "large coalition of NGOs" began to coalesce into the No-Energy Strategy.

It was co-hosted by a Canadian group called the Dogwood Initiative. Their newsletter tells us this much:

> Participants came from the Yukon, Alberta, BC, Ontario, Alaska, Montana, Colorado, Wyoming, New Mexico, Louisiana and Maine. They have been fighting the impacts of the oil industry on their communities and environment. Traditional approaches like community organizing, government relations, legal challenges and public education have served them well. All agree, however, that new tools are needed.
>
> Financiers – whether they are shareholders, banks, insurance companies or other entities – are risk averse, and we have strategies to enhance risk to create leverage.
>
> We gathered experts who have successfully used these strategies – experts on financing and corporate research, shareholder activism, credit ratings and corporate dialogue. Our experts were drawn from a "who's-who" of successful corporate campaigners. *Friends of the Earth* and *Rainforest Action Network* sent trainers, and people from *AmazonWatch* and the *Burma Project* were involved in the preparation.
>
> The coming months should be very interesting, as the foundation is put in place to hit one target corporation's operations across North America – creating political risks, threatening their social licence and right to operate, launching lawsuits, and educating investors, bankers, credit raters and insurers on undisclosed liabilities.

Charming folks, these Energy Killers. This appears to be just about where the author of the NoDOG memo began to have second thoughts, although it took him (her?) more than another year to actually convey it to our source.

It must have been too much for him to watch his friends shift from loving nature to hating corporations and lusting for power over America's energy economy. Maybe the tipping point came when he witnessed their scheming to pit one company and industry against another, in vicious combat reminiscent of Roman emperors presiding over gladiatorial battles – this time with corporate executives, employees and families as the helpless, bloodied victims.

Perhaps he could no longer stomach the sadistic glee in the eyes of OGAP/Dogwood activists, over the prospect of destroying companies and maybe even an entire industry.

Those Energy Killers need to be brought to account. They deserve the condemnation of every decent person on the planet, for they are also plying their evil trade against mining, drilling, electricity generation and economic development in Africa, Asia, Europe and Latin America.

Rights to enjoy nature – sure. But what about the basic civil rights of all these victims?

This blackmail, inhumanity and economic destruction ought to be subject to the same civil and criminal penalties that for-profit corporations would suffer for anti-trust, restraint-of-trade, espionage and sabotage, if they tried these tactics on their competitors. We need a few attorneys general and tort litigators with the smarts and cojones to bring them to justice.

America has to wake up to the silent scandal of these unscrupulous non-profit multinational activist tax-exempt corporations and their fat-cat foundation financiers libeling and destroying companies and the countless families, small businesses and communities that depend on them.

This destruction of wealth, innovation and opportunity is wrong and should be a felony.

There is no First Amendment right to conspire to destroy someone.

Beyond the network that the Oil and Gas Accountability Project and Earthworks assembled, one of those "traditional Republican constituencies and hook-and-bullet enthusiast" groups made itself known a few years ago: the Theodore Roosevelt Conservation Partnership (TRCP).

Its motto is "guaranteeing you a place to hunt and fish."

I'm sure it's nice to know that you have a place to enjoy yourself – and I certainly support hunting and fishing. But would I want that guarantee to come at the price of America's energy independence, a widening Energy Gap, and countless Americans losing their jobs, their homes, their energy and economic civil rights? Would you?

Would you knowingly become a hired gun for some fancy Energy Killer group that *guaranteed* you a place for your sport? Wouldn't you ask *how* they could do that? Wouldn't you be just a little embarrassed (maybe disgusted or repulsed would be a better word), if you knew your hunting and fishing trips were obtained by harassing oil and gas providers, and kicking them off federal lands and out of business, putting their workers in unemployment lines, and then bragging about it? I know I would – and I'll bet my bottom dollar you would, too.

TRCP's foundation donors include some of the world's richest and most aggressive anti-energy "philanthropests." Here's a little box score:

Donor to TRCP	Year	Amount
Gordon E. and Betty I. Moore Foundation	2005	$600,000
The Annenberg Foundation	2005	$200,000
Turner Foundation, Inc.	2005	$450,000
Turner Foundation, Inc.	2005	$450,000
Turner Foundation, Inc.	2003	$200,000
Turner Foundation, Inc.	2002	$250,000

Gordon Moore is the co-founder of computer chip maker Intel. (Remember that next time you boot up your computer.) His personal net worth is $3.5 billion.

And that $600,000 from the Moore Mob came with the instructions that it was to be used "to change the course of energy development on public lands."

Translation: "Kill energy production on federal lands."
That's obscene.

You'll be gratified to learn that Moore Foundation president Edward E. Penhoet gets a $417,400 salary, plus $21,000 for his 401(k) account and $19,761 for healthcare benefits each year. Seventy-one other Moore employees get over $50,000 a year.

Well, Mr. Moore, Mr. Penhoet and Mr. Ted Turner, those are *my* public lands you're trifling with, *our* public lands – lands that belong to *all* Americans, who need and use *energy*.

You have no business spending enough money to support dozens of poor families for years, pressuring our government to put those resources into energy graveyards, and turning thousands of hard-working blue-collar families into beggars.

These are *people*! Have you no shame? No decency? No morals? Didn't your Mamas teach you any manners? How do you think your kids would feel if they knew you were doing this to decent American families? That you are no better than some of the people they read about in school?

Someone needs to spend $600,000 "to change the course" of the Moore Mob and its Energy Killer attitudes, by stripping them of their public tax exemption.

So TRCP has a lot of hate money from hate-filled people to do a civil-rights-killing job on your energy, and mine.

TRCP used some of that money to prepare seriously anti-energy testimony before a rigged and biased March 2007 congressional hearing.

The hearing was titled, "Access Denied: The Growing Conflict between Hunting, Fishing and Energy Development on Federal Land."

It's not a growing conflict. Hunting, fishing, energy and other a ctivities coexisted on these lands for decades. It's a *manufactured* conflict. And in reality, it's energy development that's being denied access, not hunting and fishing.

There is precious little federal land that excludes public hunting and fishing (mostly on military bases).

There's already a lot of federal land that excludes energy development. You can hunt and fish all you want on 106 million acres of Wilderness areas, for instance, but you can't develop energy there.

The kangaroo court hearing was chaired by Rep. Nick Rahall of West Virginia, a coal mining state. He was the first non-Westerner to chair the House Natural Resources Committee in living memory, and the first Democrat after 12 years of Republican control.

The hearing was really about settling old scores with the previous chairman, Richard Pombo, a Republican who favored increased energy development on federal lands and got targeted by vicious eco-groups during the 2006 election campaign that he lost.

One group, Defenders of Wildlife, even opened an office in Pombo's district to flog him with accusations of promoting child prostitution and sweatshop labor for *not* holding a hearing about living conditions in the Marianas Islands, an American Territory in the Pacific. (I'm not making this up.)

The greens spent nearly $3.5 million defeating Pombo – and millions more defeating his congressional compatriots, and giving the Democrats their new majority and Rahall his new chairmanship. (Their tax-exempt status at work. Your tax dollars at work.)

Rep. Rahall didn't forget his debt. He showered greens with comfy jobs on his committee staff, including activists from groups that worked the 2006 campaigns. Two of three senior policy advisers, Lisa James and Laurel Angell, hail from Defenders of Wildlife; Amelia Jenkins comes from the "Forest Service Employees for Environmental Ethics" (its eco-zealot membership couldn't care less about *human* ethics); staffer Wendy Van Asselt came from the Wilderness Society and Meghan Conklin moved from Greenpeace. Other Rahall recipients came from the Sierra Club, Ozone Action and other green groups. They all have Energy Killer mentalities.

Rep. Rahall has sponsored a number of bills about energy. To call them "energy bills" would be an insult to the English language. Critics aptly call them No-Energy Bills. This West Virginian is pushing America as hard and fast as possible dead into a yawning Energy Chasm.

The Theodore Roosevelt Conservation Partnership sprouted an affiliate in 2007 called the Union Sportsmen's Alliance – a group of 20 labor unions (below) that ceremoniously gave TRCP a check for $1.2 million to show their appreciation for guaranteeing them a place to hunt and fish. You can guess how many of their rank and file members will ever get to hunt and fish on these lands. But their bosses probably will, courtesy of Rahall and the Alliance. (Can you imagine Teddy Roosevelt tolerating any of this? The nerve of them to use his name!)

International Union of Bricklayers & Allied Craft Workers

International Brotherhood of Boilermakers, Iron Ship Builders, Blacksmiths, Forgers & Helpers

Utility Workers Union of America

Operative Plasterers & Cement Masons International Association

International Union of Elevator Constructors

United Mine Workers of America

United Union of Roofers, Waterproofers, & Allied Workers

International Association of Heat, Frost Insulators, & Asbestos Workers

Brotherhood of Railroad Signalmen

United Steel Workers of America

International Brotherhood of Electrical Workers

International Association of Machinists and Aerospace Workers

American Postal Workers Union

United Association of Plumbers & Pipe Fitters

International Association of Fire Fighters

Sheet Metal Workers International Association

International Association of Bridge, Structural, Ornamental, & Reinforcing Iron Workers

Bakery, Confectionery, Tobacco Workers and Grain Millers International Union

International Union of Painters & Allied Trades

Transportation Communications International Union

I suspect the whole scheme was a move to lure National Rifle Association members, who tend to vote for Second Amendment-supporting Republicans, and con them into joining a Democrat-voting organization by guaranteeing them a place to hunt. But the Union Sportsmen's Alliance is utterly silent on gun control and says nothing about gun rights, only about hunting rights.

It's not the same thing.

The vast majority of hunters use long guns – rifles and shotguns – not handguns. The Union Sportsmen's Association talks big about hunting rights, but doesn't even mention handgun rights. Long gun hunting rights and handgun rights are *definitely* not the same thing. Certainly not in inner-city America, where your right to self defense with a handgun can mean the difference between life and death.

In my view, the Theodore Roosevelt Conservation Partnership and its Union Sportsmen's Alliance are NoDOG front groups – frauds. It's hard for me to imagine that either one would ever take up arms (even a water pistol) against a single bill in the Democrat armory of gun control laws that keep flooding Congress. I don't think it will take gun owners long to figure out that TRCP and the Alliance are just another Democrat gun control group, but with an outdoorsy face – and an energy killer, job-killer agenda, to boot.

In mid-2007, another phony front group appeared: the "Sportsmen's Alliance for Responsible Oil and Gas Development."

The three founding members of this new companion of NoDOG's "large coalition of NGOs" hailed from Washington, DC: the Theodore Roosevelt Conservation Partnership, Trout Unlimited and the National Wildlife Federation.

They're all long-time partners with another unaccountable anti-energy outfit called the Environmental Working Group. Their ideologies, track record, capabilities and financing are well known, and ominous. The Alliance's message was as direct as it was reprehensible: *kill* energy production on federal lands.

The National Wildlife Federation has an annual budget of $99 million, and its agenda is a lot less supportive of hunting and fishing than it was just 20 years ago. NWF president Larry Schweiger has spent his whole career in non-profits, but gets a $250,016 salary, $15,699 benefits package and $1,813 expense account; 181 employees make over $50,000 a year.

Trout Unlimited has a $20 million annual budget. Trout president Charles Gauvin gets $201,400 in salary and $22,366 in benefits; 31 employees rake in over $50,000 a year.

The Theodore Roosevelt Conservation Partnership's annual budget is $3.4 million. President Matt Connolly has a $97,500 salary, and 6 TRCP employees get over $50,000 a year.

Environmental Working Group has an annual budget of $3.5 million. EWG president Ken Cook gets $192,593 and $8,813 in benefits; 14 EWG employees get over $50,000 a year.

A helpful insight into the mindset and ideologies of these Energy Killers appeared in a 2007 Wilderness Society booklet titled *Natural Dividends: Wildlands Protection and the Changing Economy of the Rocky Mountain West*. It reflects the self-righteous attitudes of these rich, insulated, lily-white elites. Read it carefully.

> Contrary to a common misperception, the economy of the American West no longer depends solely on traditional resource-extractive industries. Mining, logging, oil and gas development, farming and ranching are waning in importance. Instead, economic health and sustainable growth often are tied to the protection of the region's abundant natural resources – a trend that will likely intensify in the coming years. Public lands, particularly protected lands which provide natural amenities and open spaces, are crucial to this economic equation.

What does this really say?

It says the misperception is *theirs*.
These industries are still vital to the West and to America, but they want those industries *out*.

It says rich white retirees, wealthy celebrities and fancy-free heirs living on daddy's money are flocking to the American West and want it all to themselves. They can't stand seeing drilling rigs, oil and gas fields, mines, timber cutting or even ranching operations, no matter how small, in "their" backyards – or even *knowing* such things, and such people, are out there someplace.

The Wilderness Society makes it clear that their self-centered elites are giving lots of money to groups that want to keep the rabble out, and kill off the extractive industries, which are waning only because these people are deliberately strangling them – not because the resource is declining in value, potential or importance.
You could call it cultural, industrial and ethnic cleansing.

The Wilderness Society also makes it clear that the Energy Killers are pressuring legislators to do things the elites' way, remember where their campaign contributions and volunteers come from, make the "right decisions" when it's time to vote on pushing everybody but them off the public lands.

Finally, the Wilderness Society says that we members of the rabble better learn to love hiking and eating scenery, because that's about all that's going to be left for us in a few more years.

It's easy to see why these "non-profit" Energy Killers don't care about you or me. They don't have to. They've got it made, and they're out to "save the planet."

You're going to have to *make* them care about you, your civil rights, your hopes and dreams, and the companies that employ you and support your communities.
You're going to have to *make* them understand the shocking truth: they are not the sole owners of these public lands and resources, the sole arbiters of how they are used, for whose benefit.
You also own these public lands and resources.
We *all* do.
We all have a right to be heard, and listened to.
There are a lot more people who use energy than there are members in these radical environmental groups.
It's time that we also made our voices heard.

It's time that a few busloads of Black, Latino and blue-collar protesters from inner-city Denver and other places show up at the Energy Killers' gated neighborhoods and demand that they stop violating people's energy and economic civil rights.

It's time we demand they stop trying to force us to give up our real energy in exchange for illusory energy.

It's time that a few folks told off these environmental elitists:

We're sick and tired of you leading pampered lives – and then relegating us and millions like us to the back of the energy and economic bus.

We'll no longer tolerate your deciding our energy, job, transportation, heating and economic future for us. We demand a seat at the decision-making table.

We're fed up with you locking up our coal, oil, natural gas, timber and minerals ... and never even giving us a chance to figure out how many billions of dollars, and thousands of jobs, and countless wrecked lives your actions are going to cost us – before you jam it down our throats.

We really appreciate the tremendous sacrifices you and your celebrity friends have been making.

Cheryl Crow will use one square of paper per trip to the ladies room.

Cameron Diaz goes to the "ladies room" in the woods, when she's on one of her *Trippin'* excursions by jet and helicopter to savor the "cute, eco-friendly indigenous lifestyles" of impoverished Third World countries for a couple hours each month.

Cate Blanchett has promised to wash her hair less often in her new $10-million Australian mansion.

Leonardo DiCaprio is replacing his incandescent light bulbs with mercury-enhanced (!) compact fluorescent bulbs.

And Al Gore is forcing himself to endure hours onboard private jets, spewing out tons of greenhouse gases, so that he can earn hefty fees warning us about an "imminent climate crisis."

But meanwhile, your Energy Killer policies are driving up our energy costs, forcing us to choose between heating and eating and paying the mortgage, sending us to the unemployment lines and welfare rolls, and forcing us to leave lands that were ours for generations.

$1,500 a year in higher gas and electricity costs isn't much to you rich folks. It's about 0.05% of a $3,000,000 annual take in salaries, dividend checks and trust fund disbursals.

But it's almost 4% of the gross annual salaries that we earn by the sweat of our brows, working 40 to 80 hours every week. Where are we going to find an extra $1,500 a year?

We're sick and tired of that, too.

Your anti-energy, anti-insecticide, anti-biotechnology ideologies and policies have killed millions of African and other Third World babies, children and parents.

We're not going to tolerate that any more, either.

It's about time you worried less about the supposed "dangers" of modern technologies – and more about the real dangers that those technologies prevent.

It's about time you worried a little less about your own selfish desire to have America's lands and resources all to yourselves.

And a little more about the little people around you.

Now, I'll be the first to say it.

Our environment is important.

But so are people.

Environmental elitists are important, but so are little people – blue collar workers and families.

And elitists aren't nearly as important as they seem to think they are.

Come talk to us when you're ready to get real.

In the meantime, this chapter should give Energy Keepers a pretty good picture of who some of the Energy Killers are. Where some of their money comes from. How they operate. And what some of their No-Energy Tactics look like.

It also sheds a lot of light on what's really happening here:

A tough combination of incestuous relations, a limited circle of wealthy elitists, lots of political clout and connections, lots of money, and an astute, vicious No-Energy Strategy.

It's a tough combination to fight.

But that's the job of the Energy Keepers.

CHAPTER 8
FIGHTING BACK

It should be clear by now that one group – The Congress of Racial Equality (CORE) – can't fight back alone, not with a threat this large.

What do we do about that?

The answer is pretty obvious: We form a network of like-minded people, our own "large coalition of NGOs."

I think we need an Energy Keepers Network.

Exactly what that looks like I honestly don't know, but I can envision a kind of civil rights coalition that cuts across partisanship, across racial and ethnic boundaries, across religious and cultural divides, across economic and social class differences, across all the things that tend to separate us.

That's how we won the earlier civil rights struggle – which also took on seemingly insurmountable odds and all-powerful opponents. It's how we can win the new civil rights battle.

If there's one thing every human being on Earth shares, it's the need for energy. It's our Master Resource.

That makes all of us part of the Energy Keepers Network, whether or not we realize it. We were part of it long before anybody ever gave it a name.

Ironically, even the most committed, ideological, indoctrinated, self-righteous Climate Cultist needs energy. We just disagree on how much we need and how to get it.

It's that disagreement we have to bridge.

That will take diplomacy and it will take battle, just like all the civil rights conflicts of the past.

It's the battle that's the hard part.

You can look at the Energy Keepers - Energy Killers situation as a war between two networks. A "netwar," as PR experts call it, between the Energy Killers Network and the Energy Keepers Network.

Wars are usually fought over resources and access to resources. The war against the Energy Killers is no different.

It's about economics. A lot of people think economics is about money.

It's not.

Economics is about the allocation of scarce resources to individual needs and wants.

Read that again. *The allocation of scarce resources to individual needs and wants.*

The Energy Killers are waging war to allocate American energy resources on American public lands to their individual wants – to the exclusion of other people's wants and most fundamental needs.

We Energy Keepers have to defy them first, then press our demands, then stop them from monopolizing America's public lands – and finally bring them to a standstill.

They must – and they will – heed our demands.

Energy Killers think that just because they have big groups, big revenues, big memberships, and big agendas – they own the public lands.

They don't.

We own them too.

We Energy Keepers own every square inch of America's public lands – one-third of the nation – just as much as the richest grant-maker, the proudest green-group executive and the most power-hungry politician.

If we have to fight them for it, we will.

If we have to use their own tactics against them, we will.

If we have to set up Web sites and ask for public support and take public donations, we will. Think about www.energykeepers.org.

If we have to go begging to foundations and corporations for money like they do, we will.

Corporations? Big bad Corporations?

Give me a break! Even the Energy Killers' most strident, vocal, anti-corporate advocates are total hypocrites, even the ones that say they take no corporate money.

If they take foundation grants, they're taking corporate money.

Even PBS icon and Energy Killer Bill Moyers, president of the Schumann Center on Media and Democracy, Inc. – which is in fact a private foundation despite its somewhat misleading name – gives away nothing but corporate profits – the dividends from its $52 million corporate stock investment portfolio. And what's in that portfolio? Among others,

- 1,600 shares of Anadarko Petroleum,
- 3,900 shares of Arch Coal;
- 2,572 shares of ChevronTexaco;
- 2,000 shares of British Petroleum;
- 2,980 shares of ExxonMobil;
- 10,000 shares of Noble Affiliates (oil & gas);
- 10,200 shares of Pioneer Natural Resource Company (oil & gas);
- 10,000 shares of Royal Dutch Petroleum Company (Shell Oil); and
- 10,000 shares of Shell Transportation and Trading Company (Shell Oil).

There's nothing but corporate stock in Mr. Moyers' portfolio. All those prissy holier-than-thou groups that get his money are on the take from Big Oil, including *The Nation* magazine and *Washington Monthly,* which are not noted for their love of corporate America.

So don't give me any grief over Energy Keepers taking "tainted money." The only thing wrong with tainted money, in the immortal words of former Rockefeller Family Fund executive director Donald Ross, is "there 'taint enough of it."

I see an Energy Keeper Network that first of all helps the weakest, making sure that those entitled to government energy assistance get it .

I see an Energy Keeper Network that helps the disadvantaged and the poor in their struggle for independence and stability, to get off welfare, and form their own economic development councils. I've helped put such community investment organizations together and they work.

Then I see the Energy Keeper Network of the fighters, the ones who will take on the Energy Killers toe-to-toe.

I see like-minded groups coming forward and saying, yes, we're Energy Keepers too, and we work for abundant, affordable energy.

I see like-minded individuals reading this book, going to the energykeepers.org website, then signing up with Energy Keeper groups of their choice, helping spread the word, and making it their own cause.

I see other groups preparing the political groundwork, tracking votes in Congress, pressing members to vote the right way, praising those who champion abundant energy, exposing those who don't, and drafting bills that stop government grants to non-profit groups that lobby Congress.

I see public interest law firms coming to the aid of Energy Keepers across America, challenging conspiracies like the NoDOG Strategy, working for a justice system that can rein in arrogant Energy Killers.

I see public interest lobbying groups forming, changing the rules so Congress must evaluate each bill for its national energy impact – more BTUs or less, how many and what do they cost – just as the Congressional Budget Office does now with administrative costs.

I see informed citizens joining together to fight the Energy Killers, to use the Internet, to teach the Energy Reality chart and the Energy Gap, to write letters to the editor, to blog, to demand action by attorneys general, to use any means necessary to secure an energy future with real energy in it.

I see determined activists by the busload using peaceful protest, pressuring the Energy Killers to change their ways, taking the battle to them on their own turf, in conferences, in public meetings, in community councils, on college campuses, in legislative halls and congressional hearings.

I see a few brave souls confronting the Energy Killers directly, demanding they sign a pledge to refrain from any action that lowers America's energy production or raises energy prices – and holding them accountable.

I see the power of the Energy Killers fading as more Americans become Energy Keepers, winning their economic civil rights, possessing their energy rights, holding the torch of liberty high.

And I see you there in the light.

APPENDIX A
THE ENERGY KEEPERS
CODE OF CONDUCT

1. I will use energy thoughtfully, beneficially and enjoyably, seeking the most energy-efficient equipment I can afford and defending my individual choices.

2. I will not allow Energy Killers to dictate what is best for me.

3. I will support, by word and deed, individuals, companies and organizations that promote abundant, reliable, affordable energy.

4. I will not join or support any individual or group that advocates less energy production or higher energy prices, no matter how attractive they may seem otherwise.

5. I will never stop pressuring for more energy production at affordable prices, and will never compromise or abandon my energy and economic civil rights or those of others.

6. I will demand that my views on energy, climate and related political decisions be heard by policy makers, legislative bodies, the courts and the media.

7. I will confront the threats of Climate Intimidators and demand respect for my opinions.

8. I will remember that science can be corrupted, and that government science can be corrupted absolutely.

9. I will not be bought off by promises of government energy welfare money, and will not let the Energy Killers turn me into a beggar at the American banquet.

10. I will take my Energy Keeper beliefs with me into the voting booth.

APPENDIX B
The Guilty Conscience Memo
"The NoDOG Memo"
("No Dirty Oil and Gas")

The memo reproduced below was given in late 2006 by an anonymous source from an environmental group to another anonymous source in the petroleum industry who circulated it among executives and key government officials.

Because of its shadowy origin, its contents have been closely examined by several experts who believe it to be an authentic document from an insider whose colleagues had crossed moral boundaries the source could not tolerate.

Considering that the memo appeared in 2006 and that its predictions for 2007 came true, there is little doubt that it is a reliable description of secret plans that actually came from within the environmental movement.

However, as with all documents of uncertain origin, it must be taken with a degree of caution and skepticism.

It is reproduced here verbatim as background for Chapters 6 and 7. The only edits are clearly identified by brackets [...] to supply definitions for technical terms.

Grassroots Opposition to Oil and Exploration and Production in the U.S. West (2007-2008).

A large coalition of NGOs has coalesced around a six year strategy to reform the operations of the oil and gas industry in the United States. This strategy includes the current emphasis on climate change but increasingly will focus on oil and gas operations in the U.S. West. The highlight of the activities in the coming years will be an overarching, multi-issue strategy focused on terrestrial oil and gas operations [non-offshore].

Two major elements of the strategy will focus on New Mexico, where Governor Richardson has hinted that he will run for the Presidency in 2008. Environmentalists believe that they build campaigns that play into Richardson's ambitions and win support for numerous state-wide initiatives that would hamper oil and gas development in the state. Winning specific legislation in Colorado is the coalition's second-highest state priority.

Finally, outside of the context of the larger Mountain West strategy, the groups will also begin to push in earnest for the protection of specific places, starting with Valle Vidal in New Mexico, with the intention of building support for increased lands protection in many other areas, such as parts of the Alaska Strategic Petroleum Reserve and Wyoming.

NoDOG.

At the center of the Western campaign is a new effort, currently referred to as No Dirty Oil and Gas or NoDOG. The NoDOG strategy is a three-year plan designed to win a complete restructuring of the laws governing terrestrial oil and gas operations. Among the key issues that the strategy plans to address is what the activists call the degradation of public lands, the use and liberation of toxic metals and chemicals in oil and gas operations, drilling wastes treatment and surface owner protection.

The strategy has two elements. The first is a series of state-based campaigns. These campaigns will advocate specific pieces of state legislation, each of which will address one of the priority region-wide issues. The passage   of one of these state laws – such as a surface owners' protection in New Mexico – will be used by members of the coalition in other states to justify a similar state law. According to this strategy, once a number of states have passed such laws, national groups will argue that the federal government should harmonize the statutes.

In parallel with the state campaigns will be a market campaign. The campaign will not focus on a specific target until 2008, buts its goal will be to win major concessions from one or two major oil and gas operators in the West. These concessions will form the basis for a code of conduct that will be offered in the industry. The campaign figures that if two or three companies sign on to the code of conduct, it will weaken industry's hand at the state level and in Congress, as some in the industry will be on record supporting elements of the NoDOG legislative proposals.

NoDOG Market Campaign – Phase One.

NoDOG's first phase, which will begin in January, will take one year and will focus on bringing attention to the environmental effects of oil and gas operations. The first phase will look like a traditional public interest information–awareness campaign, but its end goal will be to establish a baseline set of standards for oil and gas operations. Over the following two years, specific oil and gas operations and corporations will be held to this standard. Companies will be asked to meet the standard or improve upon it or face a market campaign (public attacks on the company from a broad coalition of NGOs).

In 2007, the organizations involved in the campaign will:

• Launch a new corporate campaign website (www.nodog.org has been taken, so they are looking for another site name).

• Issue a report outlining problems with current oil and gas operations.

• Recruit "victim groups" who can be profiled in the report and who can be called upon the testify at the state and federal level.

• Broaden coalition to increase the number of traditional Republican constituencies and hook-and-bullet enthusiasts.

• In a media campaign, publicize the relationship between the negative effects of oil and gas operations and specific products, including gasoline and plastics.

By the end of 2007, the goal of the market campaign aspect of the NoDOG strategy is to have increased the perception nationwide that oil and gas operations cause environmental damage, health effects (particularly to children) and generally anger local residents. The goal is to set the stage for a corporate campaign, where a single specific corporation (not yet identified) will be singled out as causing a litany of health and community problems in the West.

NoDOG State campaigns in 2007.

In the state element of the NoDOG strategy, OGAP has determined three priority state battles, two in New Mexico, one in Colorado.

New Mexico – Surface Owners Protection.

In New Mexico, a broad coalition of national, regional and local groups will join to press for the passage of the Surface Owners Protection Act and to win a ban on unlined production waste pits.

OGAP member groups have built what they consider to be a close alliance with the New Mexico Cattle Growers Association to support the surface owners protection bill. OGAP has not yet finished drafting the final bill that they will push for the legislature and governor to support, but the group is already looking into ad buys to December and January to urge New Mexicans to call or email their legislators and demand surface owner protection. The ads will be augmented with public service announcement that will run on the radio and television in what they determine are "priority communities." Together the activists hope that this will continue to spur demand inside the legislature for a surface owner protection bill.

In support of the bill once it is introduced, the coalition will continue to take out ads in key areas. Crucial to this campaign will be to update the group's comparison of the proposed New Mexico bill to those surface owner protection bills that have already passed. Finally, they will pay particular attention to surface owner protection laws in Wyoming and Oklahoma, and depending on what the conclude, will use these either to bolster their effort or to show what "watering down" of the OGAP proposal would do.

The key area in New Mexico where OGAP has focused its media attention in the past are:

- Colifax.
- Framingham (city).
- Carlsbad (city).
- Otero.
- Rio Arriba.

These are the likely areas of focus for the 2007 public service announcements and ad buys, but this is not yet certain.

New Mexico – Unlined Production Waste Pits.

OGAP and its allied groups will call on New Mexico to:

- Ban the use of unlined production waste pits.
- Require companies to test their pit wastes and dispose of hazardous waste in "appropriate" facilities.
- Require closed loop systems in areas with groundwater close to the surface.

OGAP will fight for these three elements as part of one single strategy on drilling wastes in the state. The coalition plans to use the state Oil Conservation Division's public meetings as the chief venues for bringing their objectives to the state's regulators, the media and the public.

In support of their testimony at these public meetings, the coalition will issue a report in March that will contend that current industry disposal practices has led to significant groundwater contamination. In addition to the report, they will find spokespeople from communities in the Southeast and Northwest parts of the state, who will provide "first hand" stories of the contamination that can be caused by current disposal practices.

Throughout the year, the coalition will also bring attention to forthcoming studies by longtime oil opponent Wilma Subra and by environmental health advocate Theo Colburn. Both activists will be held out as "experts" – Subra in the basics of oil and gas operations and waste disposal: Colburn on the health effects of exposure to certain chemicals used in oil and gas operations.

In addition to the reports and testimony by these two experts, the coalition will take out ads in the Santa Fe and Albuquerque newspapers focused on the need for the state Oil Conservation Commission (OCC) to address disposal issues.

Finally, near the end of the year, the coalition wants to set the stage for a series of expert reports and testimony for the OCC hearing on disposal rules. The activists expect this meeting in the late-fall 2007.

Colorado – Right to Know.

Arguing that no agency regulates the public health impacts of the chemicals used and released during oil and gas development in the state, OGAP and its allies will press for a law that will require companies to disclose the chemicals they use during oil and gas extraction. This effort will build on a similarly themed campaign in 2006 in which the coalition called on the state Department of Health and Environment (CDPHE). The goal in 2007 is to turn the rhetorical battle of 2006 into actual regulation.

The primary strategic objective is to win passage of legislation that would explicitly give CDPHE authority to demand disclosure and monitoring of chemical releases in the oil and gas industry. A second goal is to have the legislation demand that CDPHE develop rules that would prevent negative health impacts from oil and gas operations.

The coalition plans to bring attention to the chemicals used and liberated during oil and gas operations. They will release a report, likely written by Theo Colburn, on the health impacts of these chemicals, and it will pay particular attention to those chemicals that are banned in Europe but still allowed for use in the United States. This report will also discuss the primary ways that Coloradoans come into contact with these chemicals.

In support of the issue, OGAP and its allies will try to win (and publicize) the endorsement of local and statewide public officials, who will pledge to support the expansion of CDPHE's authority. The coalition is also looking to recruit nurses and others from the health field to act as spokespeople, rather than relying solely on familiar environmental advocates.

Once local political figures and some health professionals have agreed to speak out on the issue of the health effects of chemicals used in oil and gas operations, the coalition will begin to publicize their demands in earnest. They will to buy ads and place public service announcements in various media across the state. The coalition will also begin to work with the editorial boards of the Denver Post, Rocky Mountain News, Durango Herald, Glenwood Post and Grand Junction Daily Sentinel. The coalition hopes to begin their recruitment efforts in mid-December and to begin bringing public attention to the proposal legislation in mid-January.

NoDOG – The Longer Term.

The goal of the NoDOG strategy in 2007 is to introduce the concept that oil and gas operations have negative consequences for surface owners and for public health. OGAP and its allies believe that if they are able to simultaneously bring national attention to the West as an environmental battleground and also pass two of the three major state efforts into law, they will have a solid platform from which they can begin their second phase.

The highlight of the second phase will be the distribution of a code of conduct for the industry. The code of conduct will encompass a number of existing state laws, and companies that sign on will agree not to use the proscribed methods in any state – not just those where it is illegal. Meanwhile, the activists will single out one of the major players in the industry as a particularly bad actor. This target will receive considerable negative publicity that the activists will both distract corporate leadership and which they hope to use to make permitting more difficult for the company that has been singled out.

By 2009, the coalition hopes to have led at least one company to have signed on to the code of conduct. It will then present the code of conduct and a selection of new state laws together to Congress as the basis for the argument that the federal government is far behind industry and the states in protecting the public from oil and gas operations. The market campaign and the state laws, then, will together form the basis for a new federal law governing oil and gas.

BIBLIOGRAPHY

Ron Arnold, "NoDOG Strategy Effective and Insidious," *American Oil and Gas Reporter*, Vol. 50, No. 11, November 2007, pp.44-46.

Ron Arnold, *Freezing in the Dark: Money, Power, Politics and The Vast Left Wing Conspiracy*, Bellevue, Washington: Merril Press (2007).

Jesse H. Ausubel, "Renewable and Nuclear Heresies," *International Journal of Nuclear Governance, Economy and Ecology*, Vol. 1, No. 3 (2007), pp. 229-243.

Dennis T. Avery and S. Fred Singer, *Unstoppable Global Warming: Every 1,500 Years,* Lanham, MD: Rowman and Littlefield Publishers (2007).

Ronald Bailey (editor) and Competitive Enterprise Institute, *Global Warming and Other Eco Myths: How the Environmental Movement Uses False Science to Scare Us to Death*, Roseville, CA: Prima Lifestyles (2002).

Wayne E. Baker, *America's Crisis of Values: Reality and Perception*, Princeton, NJ: Princeton University Press (2005).

Robert L. Bradley, Jr. and Richard W. Fulmer, *Energy: The Master Resource – An Introduction to the History, Technology, Economics and Public Policy of Energy*, Dubuque, IA: Kendall/Hunt Publishing Company (2004).

John Brignell, *Everything Is Caused By Global Warming: 600 Web links to everything under the sun*, online at www.americanthinker.com/blog/2007/11/everything_is_caused_by_global.html

Bonner Cohen, *The Green Wave: Environmentalism and Its Consequences*, Washington, DC: Capital Research Center (2006).

Michael Crichton, *State of Fear*, New York: HarperCollins (2004).

Andrew E. Dessler and Edward A. Parson, *The Science and Politics of Global Climate Change: A Guide to the Debate*, New York: Cambridge University Press (2006).

Elaine Dewar, *Cloak of Green,* Toronto, ON: James Lorimer & Company (1995).

Jack W. Dini, *Challenging Environmental Mythology: Wrestling Zeus*, Raleigh, NC: SciTech Publishing (2003).

Paul Driessen, *Eco-Imperialism: Green Power Black Death*, Bellevue, WA: Free Enterprise Press, (2003).

Douglas Dupler (editor), *Conserving the Environment: The opposing viewpoints*, New York: Greenhaven Press/Thomson Gale (2006).

Martin Durkin, *The Great Global Warming Swindle*, WAG-TV and Channel Four, London (2007).

Holly Fretwell, *The Sky's Not Falling! Why It's Ok to Chill About Global Warming*, Los Angeles, CA: World Ahead Publishing (2007).

Al Gore*, An Inconvenient Truth: The Planetary Emergency of Global Warming and What We Can Do About It*, Emamus, PA: Rodale Books (2006).

Michelle Haefle, Pete Morton, Nada Culver, *Natural Dividends: Wildland Protection and the Changing Economy of the Rocky Mountain West*, Washington, DC: The Wilderness Society, September 2007.

Howard C. Hayden, *The Solar Fraud: Why Solar Energy Won't Run the World*, Pueblo West, CO: Vales Lake Publishing (2005).

Robert Higgs and Carl Close (editors), *Re-Thinking Green: Alternatives to Environmental Bureaucracy*, Oakland, CA: The Independent Institute (2005).

Christopher C. Horner, *The Politically Incorrect Guide to Global Warming (and Environmentalism)*, Washington, DC: Regnery Publishing, Inc. (2007).

John Houghton, *Global Warming: The Complete Briefing*, New York: Cambridge University Press (2004).

Orrin C. Judd, *Redefining Sovereignty: Will liberal democracies continue to determine their own laws and public policies or yield these rights to transnational entities in search of universal order and justice?* Hanover, NH: Smith and Kraus, Inc. (2005).

Richard A. Keene, *Skywatch West: The Complete Weather Guide,* Golden, CO: Fulcrum Publishing (2004).

Marcel Leroux, *Global Warming – Myth or Reality? The Erring Ways of Climatology*, New York: Springer (2005).

Bjørn Lomborg, *Cool It: The Skeptical Environmentalist's Guide to Global Warming*, New York: Knopf (2007).

Amory B. Lovins, E. Kyle Datta, Odd-Even Bustnes, Jonathan G. Koomey, and Nathan J. Glasgow, *Winning the Oil Endgame: Innovation for Profits, Jobs, and Security*, Snowmass, CO: Rocky Mountain Institute (2005).

Jarol B. Manheim, *Biz-War and the Out-of-Power Elite: The Progressive-Left Attack on the Corporation*, Mahwah, NJ: Lawrence Erlbaum Associates, Publishers (2004).

Patrick J. Michaels, *Meltdown: The Predictable Distortion of Global Warming by Scientists, Politicians and the Media*, Washington DC: Cato Institute (2004).

Patrick J. Michaels, *Shattered Consensus: The True State of Global Warming*, Lanham, MD: Rowman and Littlefield Publishers, Inc. (2005).

Neal Morris, *Global Warming (What If We Do Nothing?)*, Strongville, OH: World Almanac Library, (2007) [children's book, ages 9-12].

National Center for Policy Analysis, *A Global Warming Primer*, Dallas, TX: National Center for Policy Analysis (2007).

National Petroleum Council, *Facing the Hard Truths About Energy*, Washington, DC: National Petroleum Council (2007).

Nick Nichols, *Rules for Corporate Warriors: How to fight and survive attack group shakedowns*, Bellevue, WA: Free Enterprise Press (2001).

Marita Noon, *Environmental Utopia*, Albuquerque, NM: Citizens Alliance for Responsible Energy (2007), available online at www.responsiblenergy.org.

Al Sonja Schmidt, *Deb and Seby's Real Deal on Global Warming,* AuthorHouse: Bloomington, IN (2008) [children's book, ages 9-15].

Julian L. Simon (author), Herman Kahn (editor), *The Resourceful Earth: A Response to Global 2000*, Boston: Blackwell Publishing (1984).

Spencer R. Weart, *The Discovery of Global Warming (New Histories of Science, Technology and Medicine)*, Cambridge, MA: Harvard University Press (2004).

Juan Williams, *Eyes on the Prize: America's Civil Rights Years, 1954-1965*, New York: Penguin (1988).

Juan Williams, *My Soul Looks Back in Wonder: Voices of the Civil Rights Experience,* New York: Sterling Publishing Company, Inc. (2004).

Daniel Yergin, *The Prize: The Epic Quest for Oil, Money and Power*, New York: Free Press (1991).

INDEX

PRAISE FOR ENERGY KEEPERS - ENERGY KILLERS

Energy Keepers - Energy Killers is the *Art of War* of this millennium. It brilliantly analyzes the politics of energy, and the ways public policies can affect the civil rights of all Americans. I strongly recommend it to anyone who wants to understand the relationships between energy, economic opportunity and environmentalism. Roy Innis is to be commended for his objective, scholarly discussion of energy, economics, climate change and the future of this great nation.

John Meredith
Project 21 and the Meredith Advocacy Group

Energy Keepers hits the nail on the head. Roy Innis' book is a must-read. Coming to grips with Energy Gaps and other issues raised in this book is vital, if we care about our children and grandchildren and the kind of world we'll leave them. There's no evidence that burning fossil fuels will cause catastrophic climate change. And the only petroleum shortages we face are politically induced. Fossil fuels must continue to play a dominant role, if we are to safeguard our poor and elderly, and encourage economic opportunity in the United States and around the world.

60 Plus Association
James L. Martin, President
Pat Boone, National Spokesman

Roy Innis has given us an inconvenient sleuth into the world of the modern day environmental movement! Even for people who never thought energy could be interesting, Energy Keepers - Energy Killers is a great read!

Every parent who cares about the future of their children should check out this book. It kicks butt, names names – and it's long overdue! If every American would read any one chapter, a new civil rights movement would definitely emerge!

I'd love to see one Energy Killer forced to live the lifestyle they are forcing upon others ... No energy resources, no income, only this book to pass the time.

Al Sonja Schmidt
Writer, producer and author